The Rogue Warrior®'s
Strategy for Success

Photo by Roger Foley

The Rogue Warrior®'s Strategy for Success

A COMMANDO'S PRINCIPLES OF WINNING

Richard Marcinko

POCKET BOOKS
New York   London   Toronto   Sydney   Tokyo   Singapore

POCKET BOOKS, a division of Simon & Schuster Inc.
1230 Avenue of the Americas, New York, NY 10020

ISBN: 0-671-00993-1

First Pocket Books hardcover printing June 1997

10 9 8 7 6 5 4 3 2 1

Printed in the U.S.A.

This book is dedicated to a host of key people in my life:

To my "sea daddies," who took the time to raise me, often at the end of their boots, and who still snipe at me with loving pleasure.

To my men, "the shooters," who were loyal and followed me— and who, thankfully, still stay in touch.

To my mentors, who are still patient and continue to try to counsel me.

To my friends and my family, who had to, and continue to, endure me and my roguish ways.

To my loyal fans, who never hesitate to express their real concerns and frustrations—which are the motivational stimuli for these literary efforts.

Again, a humble thank-you to Dr. Wayne B. Hanewicz, a close friend, omnipresent guru, and constant Warrior. He provided the insight and depth needed to bring this manuscript to a larger and more demanding audience. His only failure is that he has flunked death, and I am happy to recognize that spiritual and physical feat.

Acknowledgments

I want to thank those who have taken the time to make this book a fulfilling exercise. These people include:

Paul McCarthy, my editor at Pocket Books, who continues to inspire the ideas for these books, and who saw this book through to the end—one more time.

Cameron Stauth, who advised me on the book's reorganization, rewriting, and personal interpretation.

Bill Bottum, of Townsend and Bottum, Inc.

Liz Hartman, Amy Greeman, and Jennifer Meredith, who mastermind and coordinate the "Bataan death-march" that they lovingly call my Book Tour.

Once again, I want to express my continuing appreciation for the many unsung heroes who constantly demand the best of themselves, in relative obscurity. These are Warriors who do not recognize defeat, but continue to attack until their mission is accomplished.

Contents

CONTENTS

The Rogue Warrior's Rules of Engagement

1. Aim *before* you shoot, because the "Fire, Aim, Ready" method is bullshit.

2. Break the rules before they break you.

3. *Have* character, but don't *be* a character.

4. Lead from the front, where your troops can always see you.

5. Don't confuse planning with training, or talking with kicking ass.

6. Honor your boundary breakers as much as your boundary makers, because they're your point men.

7. Don't be afraid to make mistakes, because the path to glory is littered with fuck-ups.

8. Serve a greater cause than your own ego, or you'll be a one-man army.

9. Take risks—and then *more* risks.

10. Never be satisfied.

INTRODUCTION

As I mentioned in my previous book about success, *Leadership Secrets of the Rogue Warrior*, I do not pretend to be politically correct, or sensitive to the many special desires of the various segments of our society. I write only what I *know*, from experience I gained in unforgiving circumstances.

I know what it takes to be the absolute best. And I know the price that must be paid when I fail to achieve that level of perfection.

I am committed to my country, to all those who have chosen to work with me, and to all of you who are dedicated to excellence.

I seek perfection in performance, but I know what it means to make mistakes—and to pay for them.

The ideas that I present in this book worked when nothing else did. They produced results when nothing else could. They are simple, but powerful.

Think carefully about these ideas. Use them to help you find your own path, and use them as your guide to action.

But know this above all: If you *know what you want* in

every cell of your body and deep in your soul, *nothing can stop you.*

For many years, I led the world's greatest counterterrorism team—the legendary SEAL Team Six—and fought some of the cruelest and most desperate people on earth. In doing this, I learned the basic, ballbusting way *to get things done.* When you're fighting people who are trying to do as much damage to the world as possible, and who are quite willing to die for their cause, you learn to cut through the bullshit that mires most projects. You learn to *demand* success: *now.*

In a real-time counterterrorist operation, you cannot *afford* to indulge in the nonsense that seems to surround most projects in business and in life these days. If you allow things like infighting, egotism, complacency, and fear to mar a counterterrorist op, you will end up not just defeated, but dead—along with many others, including your closest buddies.

To succeed as a counterterrorist, in project after project, you've got to *eliminate* the natural human foibles that often undermine projects.

Sometimes, people tell me that things like egotism, complacency, and fear are just human nature. Well, *fuck* human nature. If you want to succeed and stay successful, you've got to rise *above* human nature.

During thirty years in the U.S. Navy—almost all of it spent either in war or in counterterrorist operations—I discovered that the weaknesses of human nature can be overcome. When your own ass is in the line of fire, you'd be amazed at how quickly you can rise above your weakness and get the job done. During those times, you don't even *think* about your weakness; you focus on your strength, and how you can use it to overcome your enemy and get your butt back home.

The only sure way to eliminate human foibles from your project is to build your project on a rock-hard foundation of positive values. You've got to have *rules* that guide your behavior and the behavior of your team as you engage against the enemy.

I call my own set of rules—which are listed at the beginning of this book—the Rogue Warrior's Rules of Engagement.

They are damn good rules. They've helped keep me alive and helped me to succeed.

They can help you, too.

They can help you to *engineer* your own success— *regardless* of the obstacles you face. Too many people today think that success is a matter of *luck*—of being in the right place at the right time, or of knowing the right person. That's bullshit. Success is the result of proper planning, training, execution, and follow-through—not *luck*. If you sit on your ass and wait for luck to bring you success, you'll die poor.

In particular, these rules can help you push a mission or project—*any* mission or project—through its various *stages*.

To fully succeed, a project has to have a clear beginning, middle, and end. If it doesn't, it's just an amorphous period of struggle that will probably peter out before you achieve your goal.

But if you break your project into stages, you'll be able to assess your progress as you go, kick ass when you fall behind, and adjust your strategies as the field of battle shifts.

There are five logical stages to any project: (1) planning, (2) training, (3) operations, (4) maintenance, and (5) *building* on what you've achieved.

Those are the five stages I broke missions into when I structured military operations. Now, as a security and business consultant, and as an author, I still break projects into those five stages. Why? *It works.*

You and I are going to march through the five stages of a mission together. We're going to do it with military precision. As we cover territory, I'm going to introduce you to my own strategies for success.

These strategies helped to keep me alive. And they're going to help make you successful.

As we slog through the stages of a mission together, you'll see that three elements are absolutely essential for the success of every project: *character, vision,* and *planning*.

Character is the single most important element in achieving success. If you don't have character, *you will fail.* A warrior, as I've said before, always stands for something larger than himself. But he cannot properly serve his cause unless he wields the power that character creates.

Furthermore, a warrior must have a *strategic vision* of what he hopes to achieve. As you struggle for success, you've got to be able to *see* and *feel* your ultimate goal—and the path that leads to that goal—just as surely as if you had already traveled that path and reached that goal.

Your vision will consist partly of your knowledge: the information you have about your industry, your competitors, your company, and your changing environment. But it will also consist, in part, of your dreams.

If you have enough character, you will be able to make your vision become real.

You won't be able to turn your vision into reality just through character alone, though. You've got to have a *plan*.

The plan you develop for implementing your vision and realizing your dreams must be thorough, realistic, and flexible. If you don't have a viable strategic plan, no amount of character or vision will keep your project from turning to shit.

Enough preamble! Let's get to work.

Are you ready to prepare for engagement in battle?

Then let's do it.

Move out!

PART 1

PLANNING TO SUCCEED—
THE ROGUE WARRIOR
WAY

CHAPTER ONE

ASSESSING YOUR MISSION:
GOALS, TACTICS, AND RESOURCES

"The highest realization of warfare is to attack the enemy's plans."

—Sun Tzu, *Art of War*

What's your goal for today? Say it, out loud, and be specific. Don't give me some *vague* horseshit. You've got three seconds. One, two, three. Say it.

Did you come up with it? If you already *had* a goal for today, hell yes, you came up with it. If you *didn't* already know your goal, you probably just stammered like an idiot. If all you did was hem and haw, the smartest thing you could do right now would be to pick up this book and smack yourself over the head with it. That way, you might *remember* rule number one of planning: *Have a specific goal every day.*

If you don't *care* enough to smack yourself, maybe you ought to just quit reading right now, return this book to the store, and let someone who's *serious* about success buy it. Then you can get back to *Gilligan's Island*, or whatever you *do* care about, and let the rest of your life drift by.

Who knows, though—maybe you'll still eke out a little success, via the Christopher Columbus School of Planning: You won't know where you're going, you won't know where you are when you get there, and you won't know where you've been when you get back.

Of course, Chris died broke. Keep that in mind.

I can assure you that I have a goal today, and it's damn specific, which means there's no room for me to fudge on it.

My goal today: Swim two miles wearing a light pack; with an elite corps of tough, young mercenaries I'm training for a corporate-sponsored mission in a jungle environment. It's going to be a bitch because the lake we're training in is nut-numbing cold. But I can flat-ass guarantee you that I'll make it across that lake.

What's the source of my tenacity? I call it "testicle fortitude." Some people call it "courage," or "commitment." It's an intangible emotion, and *many* words describe it. Whatever you call it, it lies at the heart of every successful mission.

What inspires my testicle fortitude? That's easy. I know exactly *what I want* out of my life, and I know exactly *who I am*. If you are sure about *who you are* and

1 0

what you want, it's easy to psych yourself up to achieve your goals. If you're *not* sure, it's damn near impossible.

Do you know exactly what you want and who you are? Those may sound like simple questions, but they're not. Most people have no idea of what they truly desire from life, nor do they really know what they have inside them that will enable them to fulfill that desire. Most people just float through life, waiting for things to happen *to* them. They're leaves in the wind. They're losers.

But they're not the only type of loser. Other losers *act* like they're working toward their long-term goal, but it's not really their *own* goal; it's a goal that was set for them by someone else, usually a parent, a boss, or a spouse. And because it's not really their own goal, lodged deep in their own gut, they usually don't have the drive to achieve it.

If where you're headed—in your job or your life—isn't *completely consistent* with who you are and what you want, you're just playing games. You're not really in control and therefore you can't really be sure where you're going.

If that's how you want to live, all I can advise you to do is: Walk fast and look worried. Maybe people won't realize you're a fool.

However, if you *do* know exactly who you are—your strengths and weaknesses, your loves and hates—and if you do know exactly what you want, you *will* be able to set your goals and make the plans that will help you achieve those goals. If you truly know yourself and know the organization you operate or operate within, you'll be able to make plans that are flexible, dynamic, and realistic.

None of us can predict the future, so no one can foresee exactly how his or her goals will eventually be achieved. Does that mean planning is futile and that operations should be guided on-the-fly? Hell, no. It means that planning is *indispensable,* because only through painstaking contingency planning can you prepare for every eventuality.

However, you can properly do this planning *only* by having a complete understanding of yourself, your company, your resources, and your environment. For example, when General Eisenhower planned the invasion of Germany, he had no way of knowing that the enemy would launch a major counterattack, the Battle of the Bulge, within weeks. He didn't know he'd have to completely scramble the fundamental movements of the divisions led by George Patton and Omar Bradley. But Eisenhower *did* have an ironclad goal—fighting on German soil—and he had an absolute knowledge of himself and his organization, the Allied Forces in Europe.

Eisenhower didn't "get married" to his initial invasion plan but saw planning as a continual, nonstop process, in need of constant revision. Therefore, when circumstances changed, so did his plan. Eisenhower knew that he couldn't just execute his own plan—he also had to attack the plan of his enemy.

In business today, the combination of your self-knowledge, your knowledge of your company, and your long-term goal is generally referred to as your "vision." In the military, we referred to vision as "strategy"—the long-term, grand plan that would achieve our ultimate goal. Every strategy consisted of many individual tactics. Every successful mission I ever led started with a strong, clear strategy, or vision. To create your vision, you've got to use your head *and* your heart. Your head will supply you with the basic facts of life: your assets and liabilities, the strengths and weaknesses of your competitors, the power of your alliances, and the characteristics of your market. Your heart will tell you about the intangibles: your degree of desire to succeed, the willpower you bring to the battle, the mind-set of your "troops," and the fears that can cripple and corrupt you.

To achieve a vision, you've got to do every bit as much soul-searching as fact-finding. You've got to ask yourself: What exact type of success do I desire, and what does this desire say about me and my character? Am I trying to achieve what *I* want or what other people think I should want? How will I know when I've succeeded? If you don't like the answers you get, revise your vision.

When your vision *is* on target—sensible, achievable, and personally rewarding—it will naturally inspire others. This inspiration is critically important because no one-man army ever won a war.

Believe me, all of this soul-searching and fact-finding

1 3

will be an ordeal. Before your plan is complete you'll be itching for action and sick of preparation. But don't give up! If you skimp on planning, you'll soon suffer even more.

The great military leader Sitting Bull welcomed the process of ordeal when seeking his visions. A rational and thoughtful man, he disdained the lazy "fire, aim, ready" approach. In June of 1876, Sitting Bull spent two days fasting, dancing, staring at the sun, and making himself bleed. Then he fell into a trance and emerged with a vision. The vision was a strategy for fighting the U.S. Army, and Sitting Bull soon got a chance to enact elements of the strategy when his encampment was attacked by General George Custer's Seventh Cavalry.

Sitting Bull's vision would have *betrayed* him, though, if it hadn't been based on cold, hard facts. Too many of today's leaders get pumped up on their own adrenaline and egotism and then abandon reality. They set goals and make plans that are vainglorious and suicidal, following in the footsteps of Sitting Bull's adversary, General George Custer, who *knew* on the day of his death that he was charging a larger force than his own, but did it anyway. Custer's sole intellectual rationale for the attack was the dictum that "Indians always retreat from a major assault."

Bad assumption, George!

As General Patton said, "Get the truth! Get all of the facts." If your basic assumptions are faulty, you'll be headed straight for hell, no matter how hard you work.

If you *can't* be realistic, get out of the way and let someone else lead. When Ulysses S. Grant took over the Union Army, President Lincoln expected him to ask for things that Lincoln could not deliver, as had the other commanders of the Union Army. As Lincoln put it, "I was waiting to see what his pet impossibility would be, and I reckoned it would be cavalry, for we hadn't enough horses; there were 15,000 troops near Harper's Ferry with no horses. Well, the other day, Grant sends me a letter about those very men, just as I expected; but what he wanted to know was whether he could make infantry out of them, or disband them. He didn't ask impossibilities of me, and he's the first general I have had that didn't."

Grant, in designing his strategies, understood perfectly that *resources are finite.* Accepting this fact is the first step in setting a realistic goal.

And don't forget this: *Time* is a resource. If your time line is unrealistic, you're screwed. As General George Marshall said of America's hurry-up effort to prepare for war in 1939, "When we had time, we had no money, and now that we have money, we have no time."

Another absolutely critical aspect of being realistic about your goals and subsequent plans is to *completely understand your environment.* If you're in business, you've got to know your customers, suppliers, distributors, and employees almost as well as you know yourself. Furthermore, don't ever expect to *change* them. Deal with them as they *are.* This may sound like heresy to some of you hard-charging executives who think that you can re-create the world in your own image, but that idea is pure bullshit. In real life, people are what they are, and you can only alter them a little around the edges. If you think you can change their core values and characteristics with a sweet enough carrot or a big enough stick, you're fooling yourself. If one of your subordinates is intrinsically lazy, don't try to fire him up—just *fire* him. If consumers don't like your product, don't try to change the consumers—change the product.

You can set unrealistic goals and make unrealistic plans all day long, but they'll only alienate people and drive you bankrupt.

As you can see by now, I consider planning to be the rock-bottom foundation of achieving success.

You know that cliché: If you fail to plan, you're planning to fail? The only way that got to be trite was by being so true.

Here are two scary statistics. (1) Only 20 percent of all top-level managers, according to a major survey, see their role as primarily that of a strategic planner. (2) The average business manager in America spends just 3 percent of his time thinking about the future.

Americans, quite obviously, love action and hate planning. And that's partly why American business is getting its ass kicked all around the world.

ROGUETOID: **The road to business hell is not paved with good intentions; it's paved with faulty assumptions.**

Lessons from War

"Sir!" yelled Brewster Raider from a little, piss-ant Whaler far below the deck of the tugboat I was on. "We're gonna need more men to stay with these boats, or the damn things are gonna *capsize*. Whatta we do?"

"Plan B!" I shouted over the high whine of a quickly building storm. Plan B was to leave three men in each of the Whalers, instead of just one, and to carry out our assault with a smaller force.

SEAL Team Six was greeting the new day in the blackness of 0130. Swells popped our little tug toward the sky, then dropped it so hard that when it hit bottom, it felt like somebody had thumped me in the balls. I'd discovered that you can *plan* on getting smacked in the balls as much as you want, but no matter how much you prepare for it, the feeling always catches you by surprise.

The drill on this wind-whipped night was to overwhelm the forces on a Gulf Coast oil rig. The opposing force was composed of men posing as the enemy. We were preparing for the real thing, which is bound to happen someday. Offshore oil rigs are among the world's least protected, most valuable assets. They're subject to takeover by terrorists or by opposing military forces.

This scenario may not happen until years from now, but when it *does* happen, America will respond according to the plan that we executed on that ugly night several years ago.

I looked over the railing at the Whaler, which was riding the same crazy elevator of water that was tossing the tug. I prepared to jump. In my mind, I planned what I'd do if I missed the Whaler and got pulled toward the man-eating propellers on the tug.

I jumped. . . .

Even though this was just a three-hour mission, I'd been planning it for months. The ultimate goal was to strike without warning, swarm the enemy before they could adequately respond, and present to the brass a plan that could be effectively replicated anywhere in the world, on four hours' notice.

The secondary goal was to keep people from being killed during the exercise. In my training exercises, people sometimes died because the exercises were so brutally realistic. I hated this loss of good men, and when it occurred, it made me work even harder to achieve maximum realism and zero mortality.

Storming the oil rig was one of the first operations of SEAL Team Six. Even before that operation, though, I'd had to make extensive plans just to construct the team itself.

Putting together SEAL Team Six included (1) selection of personnel, (2) selection of equipment, and (3) establishing an in-house intelligence operation.

To achieve each of these three components, I set specific goals and designed step-by-step plans.

For personnel, I wanted men with combat experience, foreign-language skills, and functional union skills. I wanted my men to be able to go almost anywhere on earth and be able to pose as plumbers or electricians while they gathered intelligence.

I also wanted them to be comfortable with what the Navy called "modified grooming standards" because I wanted them to look like the World, and not military.

To enable them to fit in with civilians, I equipped them with high-grade commercial gear, like Eddie Bauer stuff.

I also gave them toys that would make Batman jealous, like titanium hooks, each of which costs more than a used Subaru, and closed-circuit diving gear, which doesn't produce any telltale bubbles or sound.

In addition, I gave each man his *own* kit of equipment, tailored to his personal desires, so that no man could ever blame off-the-rack equipment for his failure. An important part of planning is not just to predict the *problems* you are going to have, but also to foresee the *excuses* you're going to get, and disable them in advance.

In addition, I *tested* this equipment to the ultimate degree *before* any serious exercises and replaced whatever broke with something better. Therefore, SEAL Team Six was a walking, talking R&D organization.

Even if our equipment didn't break during the testing phase, we still modified it, to extend it beyond its normal design functions. We customized the sights on our weapons, fine-tuned our parachutes, and dove our diving gear so far beyond military standards that the Navy had to change its dive tables.

I wanted all my men—officers *and* enlisted men—to know how to fly planes, but military rules forbid enlisted men from becoming pilots, on the theory that only officers are smart enough to fly. So I leased civilian aircraft and taught my men the commercial FAA standards myself. They all became proficient at everything from 727s, to helicopters, to amphibious aircraft.

For intelligence, we designed our own information-gathering network, using our own men. I wanted my questions about specific missions and installations to be answered by my own men, and not by the standard intelligence services. I distrusted the traditional Ivy League spooks because they always seemed to give me one-size-fits-all info, instead of the specific facts and figures that I needed.

As you can see, one of my essential strategies was to empower even the lowest-ranking of my men. Too often, grand designs fall apart at the ground level because the "little guys" who actually *implement* the plans are either unprepared or unmotivated. An example of this is the standard newspaper delivery system of about twenty years ago. Back then, major newspapers would expend tremendous energy, expertise, and expense producing their product, but would then depend on a crew of ten-year-olds for the crucial task of getting the papers to the customer. However, this system broke down every time some kid woke up with a sore throat. These days, most major papers hire adults, who deliver the papers by car. It costs more, but it works.

The net result of my care and feeding of my grunts, or "shooters," was that these guys would gladly march into hell for me and bite the tongue off the devil. And each of them would be *able* to do something like that because each shooter could fly, parachute, swim, and attack all by himself, if necessary. Each man mirrored the entire "machine" of SEAL Team Six, and the machine mirrored each man.

Furthermore, each man in SEAL Team Six knew exactly what our goals were—short-term, midterm, and long-term. All of them shared the same vision of working in a flexible, realistic, and antihierarchical team. I made sure that each of them knew who he was and what was expected of him.

When SEAL Team Six finally became fully operational and was ready for the mission against the oil rig, I devised a detailed logistical plan. In broad terms, the plan was: (1) Navigate to the rig via visual sighting in six Boston Whaler boats. (2) Launch two swim pairs from each of the six boats, to swim to the legs of the rig. (3) In the event that the current was too strong for the swimmers to reach the legs, or if the swimmers couldn't maintain visual contact with the legs bring the swimmers to the legs with the boats and secure the boats to the legs. (4) Climb the structure. (5) Swarm the enemy, on signal. (6) Take control of the rig, with help from reinforcements arriving via helicopter.

Built into each element of the plan was anticipation of the enemy's reaction. And for every reaction, we had a reactive plan.

However, I was sure that when the shit hit the fan,

Murphy's Law would kick in, and some of our best-laid plans would go from Plan A to Plan B to Plan Oh-Shit!

But, by God, we were as ready as humanly possible.

The second I jumped, I knew I was in trouble. The Whaler lurched away from me, and I plunged into the greasy Gulf water. I came to the surface inches away from the tugboat's screw, which was churning the black ocean white. Six hands from the boat grabbed onto me and hauled me aboard.

"Where's the goddamn *rig*?" I wheezed. The swells were too big to see over. We had to shift to an alternate navigation system and have the men on the tug guide us in via radio. They had transponders, handheld radar, and long-range night-vision devices.

We chugged toward the rig for an eternity on roller-coaster waves as hard rain spiked our eyes. When we got there, I tried to tie onto one of the rig's legs. But we were rising and falling too fast for that plan to be safe. We abandoned it and floated free.

I jumped overboard, swam to a leg, and looked up. Ten stories. I started to shimmy up. At first it was easy because the lower part of the leg was covered with barnacles. The barnacles cut me but gave me traction. Then, I hit a layer of oil, probably dribbled down the legs by the bastards who were occupying the rig. I slid down like a monkey on a greased pole.

"Back-up plan!" I yelled. My best climber hit the leg, carrying an aluminum "caving ladder." If he made it up, the rest of us could use the ladder.

He made it. He lowered the ladder. I started climbing, got fifty feet up, and felt the ladder pull out of its mooring and collapse. I hit the water ass-over-elbows and got smacked by the ladder.

Time was running out. We went to Plan C: We climbed up en masse, with each guy giving footing to the guy ahead of him. It was painful but effective.

By the time we got to the floor of the rig, we were heaving with fatigue.

I looked for the men from the other boats, but it was too black to see. That was good. It was our cover. But I was certain they were there. I trusted my men implicitly.

Overhead, I could hear the faint *whop-whop* of the copters. I was sure that in a matter of moments, the enemy inside would hear them, too.

"Blow the door!" I yelled.

Brewster Raider taped explosives to the main door of the control room. I flashed a signal flare, and men all over the rig dove for the main deck. *BRAMM!*

The door flapped open.

We pounded through the door and blasted dye-marker ammo at everybody that moved. I grabbed a guy, but he pulled open his shirt and gave me a sick grin. I jerked back. He was wired. Booby-trapped. I grabbed his hands and immobilized him. "Where's the detonator?" I growled.

"Eat shit."

I bent one of his hands in toward his wrist, hard. That was against the official rules of engagement. Like I cared.

His face went white. "It ain't on me," he blurted.

"Everybody! Hang back!" I yelled. Men stopped running. The booby-trapped guy smirked. "We're screwed," I said. I was stalling.

Moments later, one of my men walked up with the detonator. "Looking for this?" he said with a smile.

He'd been snooping for booby traps and detonators since the second he'd scaled the rig.

It was all part of the plan.

The rig was secure by 0220.

Lessons from Business, and from the Lives of Successful People

About fifteen years ago, the top management at Wells Fargo and Company had a vision of the future of banking. In their vision, the most successful banks had abandoned the banking industry's traditional reliance upon the impressive buildings that banks have always depended upon to convey a sense of security and stability.

For centuries, banks have maintained expensive, high-profile headquarters, as well as costly branch offices, to reassure customers that their money is safe and that the bank is reputable.

To the managers of Wells Fargo, this "edifice complex" no longer seemed necessary. After all, for many years, most banks had been federally insured, and the last major bank failures had occurred more than fifty years before, during the Depression.

The Wells Fargo management set a goal: divesting

Wells Fargo of many of its most expensive buildings. They would embrace a new system of reliance upon automated teller machines, outlets in supermarket cubicles, and new branches in plain vanilla, inexpensive buildings.

They devised a complex, gradual plan to institute this change to "virtual banking," relying upon increased advertising to preserve their image as a major, reliable banking institution.

The change was instituted slowly and carefully, and it led a veritable revolution in the banking industry. Wells Fargo's plan represented more than just a marketing adjustment; it actually changed the rules of engagement of the banking industry.

The change has been tremendously successful.

From 1990 to 1996, Wells Fargo stock went from $41 to $253, and the bank's 1995 earnings hit $1 billion. With a 2 percent return on assets and a 30 percent return on equity, the bank is near the top of its industry.

Wells Fargo had a vision and turned it into reality.

Another great example of superior corporate planning is the success of the Ford Taurus. The Taurus, as you may know, enjoyed the most successful debut of any car in modern history. But this success occurred only because the managers of Ford were smart enough to be flexible. Responding to changes in the economy, the Ford executives redefined their vision and then drastically altered their plans.

The Taurus was first conceived of in the late 1970s, during an era of unprecedented hikes in the price of gas.

Long-range planning indicated that by 1981, a gallon of gas would cost about $3.50. Therefore, the Taurus was slated to be a narrow, four-cylinder economy car.

At the time the Taurus was first planned, American car companies were being murdered by lighter, gas-efficient foreign cars, mostly from Japan. Foreign cars had begun to dominate the market after the American companies had failed to respond to a changing marketplace in the late 1960s and early 1970s. Determined not to get out-planned again, Ford's vision of the Taurus was that of a car that could recapture the cost-conscious, inflation-scarred consumer.

But by 1981, the price of gas was not even a buck-fifty. Back to the drawing board. Ford altered its vision of what the consumer wanted and threw out all of its work to date. The Ford execs redesigned the Taurus according to the changing realities. They broadened the wheelbase, added room for another passenger, and beefed up the engine from four cylinders to six.

Of course, altering their vision and changing the plan cost a small fortune. But it resulted in Ford making a large fortune.

Ford had the good sense to go to Plan B. Now I'll give you an example of what happens when a company gets *married* to its plans and refuses to adjust to real-time changes in the real world. Look at Wang. If you can still find them.

About twenty years ago, when office computerization was in its initial, widespread bloom, Wang ruled the market. It seemed as if every office had a Wang system, characterized by a central processor with scattered work-stations. Wang owned the hardware and the software, and Wang software worked *only* on Wang hardware. They looked unbeatable.

Wang's long-range plan was . . . more of the same. After all, the strategy was working, wasn't it? Even as late as 1980, Wang made a profit of $52 million and was growing 30 percent per year.

Then: *Boom!* The personal computer explosion. All of a sudden, PCs changed the entire equation of office automation. With PCs, anyone in an office could do his own work with his own desktop unit, and could interface outside the office more effectively than ever.

It was time for the managers of Wang to change their plan. They didn't. They clung to their old technologies and philosophies.

After several years, Wang did migrate to PCs. But in the time-accelerated universe of high tech, several years is like several geological epochs.

The company never fully recovered. In 1992, it filed for bankruptcy.

Wang's executives were piss-poor planners, and it almost destroyed their company.

Let's close this diatribe on the importance of setting goals and making plans with a story about one of the most powerful men of this century, Lyndon Baines Johnson. Love LBJ or hate him, you've got to admit he came a helluva long way for a little hick from Texas.

Much of his success stemmed from his mania for planning. He was a control freak who took the bull by the balls and molded his own destiny. His planning often extended decades ahead.

As a young congressman, LBJ was desperate to make some money because he'd grown up in a poor family and was determined to make himself wealthy. The only thing he loved more than money was political power.

Johnson went to a wealthy Texas businessman who owed LBJ a favor. The tycoon made Johnson an extraordinary offer. He would let Johnson into one of his oil well deals, for no money up front. The deal was certain to make Johnson rich.

LBJ hesitated. Then turned it down. He said making oil money would "kill him in politics."

The businessman was incredulous. *Kill* him? In Texas politics, oil money was a badge of honor.

But LBJ—wet behind the ears, barely removed from teaching high school—wasn't talking about *Texas* politics.

He was talking about the presidency.

That's planning.

LBJ didn't just make long-term plans. He made the *right* long-term plans.

ASK YOURSELF

- If you asked your three top people what your company's major goals were, would their answers be consistent?

- What is your vision of your company's future? What's your vision of your own future? Are these two visions compatible?
- Does your primary strategic plan have a clear beginning, middle, and end?

CHAPTER TWO

DICTATING THE RULES OF ENGAGEMENT

"We train young men to drop flaming gasoline on people, and yet their commanders will not allow them to write 'fuck' on their airplanes, because it's obscene. The horror. The horror."

—Colonel Kurtz, *Apocalypse Now*

"Actively and publicly hail defiance of the rules, many of which you labored mightily to construct in the first place."

—Tom Peters, *Thriving on Chaos*

If any subordinate ever tells you that he "loves a good, fair fight," fire the dumb son of a bitch on the spot.

The last thing in the world you should ever engage in is a fair fight.

Your fights should be *fixed*. The deck should be *stacked*. Every rule in the book should favor you and hamper your opponent. That's *my* idea of a "good fight."

Believe me, when you've been in as many battles as I have, you realize how hard it is to win under *any* circumstances, including those in which you have an advantage.

It's human nature to root for the underdog, but let me tell you something about the underdog. He usually gets his ass kicked. If your psyche *needs* to fight an uphill battle, satisfy that urge symbolically by playing chess against someone who's better, or by rooting for the Chicago Cubs. Just don't bring your masochistic urges to the office.

If you're going to be a winner, you've got to learn how to *set the rules* and make them work in your favor.

In the military, as I previously mentioned, there is an important concept called "rules of engagement." The rules of engagement govern the moral conduct of wars. Generally, the combatants agree on these rules at the beginning of a war.

Often, these rules of engagement prohibit barbaric activities like torture or the killing of civilians. As a rule, military rules of engagement incorporate existing, common sense dictates of human decency.

However, "rules of engagement" also has a broader meaning. To me, it can simply refer to *rules*, in general. It doesn't mean just the rules that govern my actions against the enemy but *all* the rules that govern all my actions, and the actions of everyone I'm allied with or fighting against. Some of these rules are set by my superiors, and *some are set by me*. The rest of the rules

3 1

are set by my allies or enemies, and I also have to factor them into my planning.

Maybe I'm just a born rebel, but I've often felt just as constricted by the rules set by my own superiors as by the rules set, in part, by my enemies.

Some of these "rules" are really nothing more than just convention, or even habit. These are the rules I hate most because there's often no moral reason behind them.

In business, there are definitely rules of engagement. Sometimes, these rules fit the strict military definition of rules of engagement: They are rules of moral conduct that all companies in an industry subscribe to. These rules are generally enforced by trade associations or by the courts.

Much more often, though, the rules of engagement in business conform with my broader definition of the term: They are just *rules.*

Usually, these rules were set in order to help the company succeed. They were established as a business tactic, or as a way to control the behavior of the work-force. When rules are *first* set, they usually make sense.

Unfortunately, though, rules often survive even after they *stop* making sense. *That's* when you need to change them and dictate *new* rules of engagement.

When you do try to dictate new rules of engagement, you're almost certain to meet resistance. Entrenched, enfranchised forces will oppose you. Because of this resistance, you probably won't be *able* to dictate rules that are absurdly lopsided in your favor. The best you can usually do is to set rules that give you a small advantage, or that neutralize your opponent's advantage.

If your opponent is one of the leaders in your field, he has probably already stacked the deck in his own favor. The top companies almost always set the rules of their own industries. If you're trying to fight your industry's top one or two companies—the Big Kids that have already made the playground rules—it's absolutely *imperative* that you try to change the rules. If you don't, you'll probably just lose a war of attrition because big companies with long histories generally structure the rules of their industries in ways that penalize newer, smaller competitors. Many large companies, for example, design their industries to include monolithic networks of middlemen, such as major distributors, who are controlled by the Big Kids. In this type of situation, the only way to win battles against the big boys is to change the rules of engagement, by bypassing the middlemen and direct-marketing to the consumer.

The worst mistake you can possibly make in trying to overcome established industry rule makers is to go *head-to-head* against them, in compliance with the rules they've already set. If you do that, they'll swat you like a fly. To win a game that's governed by someone else's rules, you've got to make an "end run" around their rules.

Often, though, the rules you must break to succeed aren't those imposed by your competitors but are those set by your *own company*. You may have even created the rules yourself. Don't let your own rules tie your hands. If you allow yourself to be straitjacketed by convention, company policy, or a stagnant strategy, your company will calcify and die. If you let this happen in your personal life, progress and people will pass you by, and you'll end up as just another worthless old windbag grousing about the good old days.

Sometimes, the rules your own company sets make sense initially but become obstacles as time passes and things change. However, managers often try to retain outdated rules. A *leader*—as opposed to a *manager*—will know not just *what* to change, but *when* to change it.

To succeed, you've got to keep innovating within your own company and *surprising* your competitors. One of the best things about changing the rules of engagement is that it almost always catches your competitors by surprise, and surprise is a strategy that is often essential for victory. In fact, the word *strategy* comes from the Greek *strategia,* which means "a maneuver designed to surprise the enemy."

Throughout military history, strategists have always tried to dictate the rules of engagement in order to achieve victory. For example, until the French-English battle of Crécy in 1346, the longbow had always been used as a mobile field weapon, with singly deployed archers advancing alongside infantry-type troops. This style, which endured for two hundred years, was perceived as the manly, courageous, and (for some reason) morally correct way to use the weapon. At Crécy, however, England's Edward III routed a larger French army by massing his archers at the distant rear of the battle, behind fortifications, and ordering them to fire simultaneously. Edward III was criticized as being barbaric for using this early form of "artillery," and other countries refused to emulate the style. Because of this, England enjoyed a strategic advantage in warfare for several more decades.

During the American Revolution, the Minutemen scored their first major victory by adopting a strategy—previously used by Indians during the French and Indian War—of sniping at massed English troops, guerrilla-style, from behind stone walls and trees. It was a radical departure for white men to use this Indian tactic, instead of the European style of frontal volleys. This divergence from the standard rules of engagement—which was deplored by the British as vicious and cowardly—allowed the Americans to seize an early advantage in the war.

General George Patton *always* found a way to make the enemy fight on Patton's terms. "The secret," Patton said, "is to move fast, and in a direction the enemy would never expect. The chance of loss is too great to fight a battle on a site which pleases the enemy. We will decide when and where we will kill the enemy."

Patton was equally adamant about dictating the rules of engagement within his own U. S. Army unit. He admonished his men, "Forget about Army regulations. Regulations are written by those who have never been in battle. Our only mission in combat is to win."

Obviously, the great generals have always done everything possible to dictate the rules of engagement. In your business life and in your personal life, you should never sit passively while someone else draws up the rules of the game.

If you want to win, make up your own rules and make other people play the game *your* way.

One of my favorite movie scenes dealing with this theme came from one of the *Star Trek* films. In the scene, we learn that Captain Kirk was the only person ever to win a computerized leadership game. A young commander asks Kirk how he did it. Kirk tells him that he won by breaking into the computer and changing the program. "I simply refused to lose," says Kirk, "so I changed the rules."

ROGUETOID: **Breaking the rules is "unfair" only to the person who made them.**

Lessons from War

The commander of one of America's largest nuclear submarine bases eyed me suspiciously from across the expanse of his vast, spit-shined mahogany desk. As the leader of a small, elite unit called Red Cell, I was his "enemy." Red Cell was a group of nail-tough Navy men—many of whom I had recruited from SEAL Team Six—who played the role of terrorists in real-time assaults on Navy installations, in order to test the security of the installations.

I was in this commander's office, in the New London, Connecticut, area, to negotiate the rules of engagement for our upcoming "terrorist assault" on his facility.

"First! And foremost, Captain," he barked in staccato bursts, *"when* and *where* will you deploy?"

"Due respect, sir? Negative on that. Terrorists don't reveal their plans."

He bristled and bitched. But I held my ground. Winning this issue, at this time, was far more important than the successful execution of any other single element of this maneuver. The commander blew up, ranted and raved, then gave me the silent treatment, then cooled off, then tried to kill me with kindness. Didn't work. Finally, he gave in.

"Next issue!" he yelped. "You are *not!* Repeat, not! Authorized to board nuclear submarines, or enter adjacent areas. Security clearance issue! End of story!"

Bullshit. Making his *big* toys go boom was my ultimate goal. Doom on him.

"I want you to! And this is important! *Stay away* from the private contractors around the base. Lockheed! General Dynamics! Their personnel are under the same security constraints as my men, but enforcement is problematic. So! Arm's length from them! After all, Captain, fair is fair."

Fair is *what?* "I'll do my utmost, sir." I kept a straight face. "But don't expect miracles." His eyebrows went into a hard, sharp V, but he didn't say anything. He clearly did not realize the importance of this phase of the operation. It amazed me that this man had managed to become a base commander.

By the time I left his office, I was certain that we'd already won our battle. I had controlled the rules of engagement. Now all we had to do was go through the motions of the maneuver.

The next afternoon, I rented a twenty-two-foot Bayliner ski boat and we water-skied past the base and videotaped their dry docks, which housed the nuclear submarines. No one challenged us. The base's security forces didn't even seem to notice that our boat was flying the Iranian flag.

That night, the men of Red Cell convened at an off-base bar called the Officers' Club, which was a hangout for the employees of the local defense contractors. A couple of my best-looking guys scouted out some women from General Dynamics and asked them to dance. While they were dancing, we rifled the women's purses and swiped their base clearance cards. Half an hour later, we had color photocopies of the cards. We slipped the originals back into their purses.

The next morning, we replaced the photo IDs on the women's cards with our own pictures and got the cards laminated at a local dimestore.

That evening, we mustered for a very early beer call, and I had four of my guys get blasted. I tossed my four drunks into a car and drove them to the base, to do some

3 8

sensor snooping. I stationed the four men at each of the base's four perimeters, which were walled off with chain-link fence. At 2200 hours, all four went over the fences. Three of them tripped sensors and were promptly caught. They told the security police that their stunt was the product of a barroom bet, and because they were reeling like winos and reeking of alcohol, the security force bought the story and kicked them out.

The fourth guy—who'd gone over the back wall—hadn't been noticed. *No sensors back there.* Jesus!

The next night, we struck. We all went over the back wall and then split into two groups. Raider led one group to the Ordnance Facility and the nuclear weapons preparation and inspection area. I led the other group to the lower base, where the operational subs were at the piers.

On our way to the piers, a sentry with a sidearm yelled at us to halt, but I blasted him with a silenced paint gun. According to the rules of engagement, he had to drop and shut up. We carted away his "body." We videotaped the incident, as well as the rest of the operation, to prove later on that we had achieved what we claimed.

Raider taped a timer-detonated explosive charge to a natural gas tank outside the Ordnance Facility and spray-painted *BANG* on the tank in big yellow letters. Then, inside, he found the nuclear devices and put a "bomb" next to an immense, stainless steel–sheathed nuclear torpedo. The torpedo wasn't equipped with its trigger, but the "bomb" Raider left behind was more than powerful enough to detonate it.

Using the videotaped intelligence we'd gathered during our ski boat reconnaissance, my group infiltrated the subs at the piers. Security was tighter there, but when we were challenged, we badged security with our fake IDs, and they let us pass. We boarded a sub, and I placed a simulated time bomb in a cardboard box and planted "charges" on the diving planes.

We regrouped and headed for the "nerve center" of the base—the headquarters, communications station, and records depot. These facilities were all in one six-story tower of black steel and tinted glass. We took down the four sentries at the main floor check-in station and then placed a massive radio-controlled "bomb" at the bottom of an elevator shaft.

We left through the front gate.

The next morning, I met with the base commander. He was glum.

"You had my ass whipped from the get-go, didn't you?" he asked.

"Sir, in all probability, yes. In most instances, we had the upper hand."

"And when you didn't, you cheated."

"We cheated fair and square, sir."

He hit me with a hard look. "You believe that to be acceptable Navy behavior?"

"No, sir! I believe it to be acceptable *terrorist* behavior."

He glared at me. I tried not to smile. I almost succeeded. We both knew that in the final analysis, it didn't matter if my behavior had been "acceptable." I had won. He had lost. That was all anyone would ever remember.

Lessons from Business, and from the Lives of Successful People

Lee Iacocca has often said that the Japanese "don't play according to the same rules" that guide American companies. He's right, of course. For decades, Japan has made "end runs" around the rules set by the American business establishment.

One of Japan's most fundamental and successful strategies has been to spend relatively less on research and development than American companies, and to focus instead on refining the manufacturing processes of products invented in America. This strategy has been brilliantly successful because it has allowed Japanese companies to avoid competing against America at what America does best.

Another Japanese strategy has been to place high tariffs and strict regulations on foreign imports, to protect Japanese industries. This policy has discouraged many American companies from even trying to penetrate the Japanese market. But it didn't discourage Häagen-Dazs.

In 1993, American-based Häagen-Dazs was told by Japanese customs officials that its ice cream had to go through the same ten-day inspection process that all dairy products face when entering Japan. But Häagen-Dazs ice cream responds poorly to long storage periods because its high-quality ingredients tend to spoil quickly. The ten-day wait was a disaster for Häagen-Dazs.

Instead of whining about unfair rules and giving up on the Japanese market, as had so many other American companies, Häagen-Dazs went to the Japanese Ministry of Health, which controlled the inspection process. Häagen-Dazs didn't ask for special privileges but instead offered to develop a new, more efficient inspection process for dairy products. Furthermore, Häagen-Dazs volunteered to pay for the entire cost of shifting to the new process.

The Japanese government—unaccustomed to being underwritten by foreign companies—took the deal.

Thus, Häagen-Dazs seized the initiative and successfully changed the rules of engagement.

Now Häagen-Dazs has the largest market share of premium ice cream in Japan.

Sometimes, companies achieve success by breaking the standard corporate rules of control and ownership. A notable example is Bill Bottum's Townsend and Bottum Capital Fund, based in Michigan. Many years ago, Bill Bottum structured his company to be owned, and largely controlled, by its employees. His system, which has been called "very radical" by some analysts, has been extremely successful.

Another company that changed its industry's rules is Xerox. Xerox was once just an upstart in the photocopier business, tagging after the more established 3M Company. But Xerox dictated new rules of engagement. When it entered the photocopy market, it refused to sell its copy machines, as 3M was doing, and instead leased them. 3M, however, refused to adjust to the new rules. 3M continued to sell its machines and scorned lease arrangements. Xerox took over the market.

Another high-tech company that changed its industry's rules of engagement was Dell Computer. When a nineteen-year-old boy, Michael Dell, started his own little computer company, he knew he couldn't compete with established companies for floor space in stores. However, the rules of the industry, at that time, dictated that computers *had* to be sold in stores. Every company in the industry believed that customers wouldn't trust a mail-order company to provide such a high-end item.

Michael Dell broke the rule. He direct-marketed. And he built an $800 million company in five years.

Compaq Computers also beefed up its strength by breaking the rules. In 1993, Compaq scattered its sales force, moving its salespeople away from central offices, which was the industry norm. It moved them to home offices. As a result, revenues doubled while the sales division was cut by one-third. Other computer companies soon followed the example.

An entire *industry* that owes its life to rule breaking is the biotech industry. Until a few years ago, virtually all pharmaceutical drugs were developed through the application of *chemistry*; companies tested thousands of chemical compounds to see if any of them could be used as effective medications. This approach yielded a success rate of approximately one new product for every ten thousand compounds tested. However, an innovative cadre of rule breakers created an entirely new approach, through the application of *biology*. They began to study healing substances that occur naturally in the body and then tried to mimic these substances through genetic engineering. This new approach yields a success rate of approximately one new product for every *ten* that are tested.

Breaking the most basic rule of pharmacologic research proved to be incredibly lucrative for the people who'd had the guts to do it. By the 1990s, the infant industry of biotechnology was a darling of Wall Street and made many young rule breakers rich.

To close out this section on planning and preparation, I'll tell you one last LBJ story. As you'll remember from the first chapter, Lyndon Johnson was determined, even when he was just a skinny, postadolescent congressman, to become president. The primary way he rose to the vice presidency, which of course soon vaulted him to the presidency, was to gain a reputation as America's master deal-maker. In the House, and later as senate majority leader, LBJ exhibited a remarkable ability to link opposing forces and hammer out legislation.

Many historians credit Johnson's capacity for bringing legislators together to his charm, tenacity, intelligence, and idealism. But they're wrong. That's just what LBJ *wanted* people to think.

In reality, LBJ became the master manipulator of the House and Senate by completely changing the rules of engagement that governed congressional alliances. Here's how he did it.

Shortly before the election of 1940, when Republican Wendell Willkie was in a dead heat with President

Roosevelt, Democratic candidates for Congress were desperate for campaign money. The country was becoming disenchanted with Democrats, and the prime source of Democratic fund-raising, the working class, was too impoverished by the Depression to make significant political contributions. Furthermore, the sole central source of funds for Democrats, which was controlled by the Democratic National Committee, was being gutted by the president's campaign.

LBJ, an essentially unknown, thirty-one-year old, first-term congressman, lobbied hard to become a special assistant to the Democratic National Committee. The same day he joined the Committee, he contacted several key Texas oilmen and construction tycoons whom he'd been secretly serving for several years. He told them he had a plan and implored them to send huge contributions to the DNC. They agreed to do so. Then LBJ gave the wealthy donors a list of candidates, and when they sent in their contributions, they were to specify which candidates were to receive their funds. Technically, this system of campaign finance was legal, even though it was a thinly disguised method of giving individual candidates personal contributions that far exceeded the legal limit.

Just before the funds would be dispersed to a candidate, LBJ would send the candidate a telegram that said "AS RESULT MY VISIT TO CONGRESSIONAL COMMITTEE FEW MINUTES AGO, YOU SHOULD RECEIVE AIRMAIL SPECIAL DELIVERY LETTER FROM THEM WHICH IS TO BE MAILED TONIGHT."

Some candidates got several such telegrams from LBJ during the 1940 campaign. By the time these candidates were elected, young Lyndon Johnson had become their chief benefactor.

Of course, these politicians were extremely indebted to Johnson and gladly yielded to his desires on certain legislation.

Thus, money—not charm, tenacity, nor ideology— became the wellspring of Lyndon Johnson's burgeoning political power.

LBJ's method was a clear departure from the standard congressional rules of engagement that governed deal-making. Previously, political deal-making had been achieved through similarities of ideology, through trading political favors, or through personal friendship. No congressman had ever before built a power base simply by "buying" his fellow legislators.

Johnson also used his coalition of indebted congressmen to pass legislation that favored his Texas moneymen. Thus, the source of his DNC funds was continually replenished.

This method was used by LBJ countless times over many years as Johnson moved from the House to the Senate.

Using this scheme, LBJ gained a tremendous ability to meld apparently disparate politicians on a wide variety of issues.

Throughout his career, LBJ successfully hid from the public the *real* technique that made him America's greatest deal-maker.

The American public thought Lyndon Johnson was just a great negotiator. He was more than that. He was someone who knew how to dictate the rules of engagement.

ASK YOURSELF

- Do the primary rules of engagement in your industry favor you, or your competitors?
- If the rules of your industry don't favor you, do you still follow them? Why?
- When was the last time you surprised a competitor?

PART 2

TRAINING FOR SUCCESS— THE ROGUE WARRIOR WAY

CHAPTER THREE

BUILDING A TEAM WITH CHARACTER

"Character is destiny."
—George Eliot

"Character—not wealth, power or position—is the supreme word."

—John D. Rockefeller

Around 500 B.C., the legendary military strategist Sun Tzu went to the king of his province. He told the king that he could lead the army to victory and make the king the ruler of heaven and earth. The king was intrigued. But the king insisted that Sun Tzu first demonstrate his military genius.

Sun Tzu agreed to the test. He asked the king to make him the commander of an army composed of the women of the inner palace, most of whom were the king's concubines.

The king called forth three hundred women and put Sun Tzu in charge of them.

Sun Tzu appointed the king's two most beloved concubines to be the "generals" of two companies, each composed of a hundred and fifty women.

Sun Tzu ordered the women in both companies to wear full armor and helmets, and to arm themselves with swords. He assembled them in front of all the people of the province, and told them how to march, turn, and wield their weapons. He told them that when he began to beat his drum, they should begin marching. When he said this to them, they covered their mouths and laughed.

Sun Tzu began to beat his drum, but again the women just laughed. Sun Tzu reiterated his orders. Then he again beat his drum. The women began to laugh again and could not stop.

Sun Tzu became enraged and commanded the standard military punishment for failure to obey orders: beheading of the army's "generals."

The king objected strongly. He told Sun Tzu of his love for these two women. But Sun Tzu reminded the king that the leader of the king's army, once installed, held complete power over the army.

The women were beheaded.

Sun Tzu again beat his drum. The two companies marched flawlessly.

Then Sun Tzu dismissed the women from service and requested male army volunteers from the assembled crowd.

Only the men of highest character volunteered.

Sun Tzu's army swept to many victories and made the king the greatest ruler on earth.

As you can see, Sun Tzu was one smart son of a bitch. He knew that *training begins with character*. And he knew the three most important things about character. (1) If your troops don't have character, they're just a mob. (2) Character *can* be taught. (3) It's easier to *find* people with character than to *teach* character.

In my military career, the one quality I valued most in my men was character. It was always the first thing I looked for in recruiting men for SEAL Team Six or Red Cell. I could train a skinny little runt with minimal skills to be a veritable Julius Caesar, if the runt had enough character.

If your people don't have character, you will never be able to implement your vision, your goals, or your plans. Character is the animating force that will spark life into your dreams.

Finding people who have character, and finding character in the people you have, is the first vital step in selection, and then training. If you overlook character, the rest of your training will be a charade.

As far as I'm concerned, character is composed of just two things: *strength* and *morality*.

By strength, I mean both physical and mental strength.

Physically, a guy in SEAL Team Six or Red Cell didn't need to be Arnold Schwarzenegger, but he had to be strong enough to fight until he dropped, and then be fully rested by the time he hit the floor.

Mentally, he had to be tough enough to fall asleep during root canal surgery. To be able to do something like that, a man needed not just courage—which is always an important element of mental strength—but he also needed to have the ability to focus his mind *completely* on whatever he chose. Controlling mental focus is just as important as controlling fear.

The other element of mental strength that I always looked for was a commitment to excellence. If you're a boss, you should *expect* excellence and *provide* excellence. At SEAL Team Six and in Red Cell, I did everything I could to provide my men with the best training, the best equipment, and the best strategic plan possible. Their support systems were excellent, and that was vital, because excellence *breeds* excellence, and mediocrity breeds mediocrity. It's that simple.

Another indispensable aspect of mental toughness is the willingness to occasionally suffer. Sometimes, you've got to ask yourself: Do I want to be happy today, or do I want to further my success? You can't always do both.

Now let's consider the other primary component of character: morality. By morality, I mean decency, a sense of self-responsibility, generosity, and a proper set of values.

To be part of my team, a guy had to have a gut-level feeling for basic human decency. He had to have an innate desire to always do the right thing, rather than to just blindly follow the rules.

He also had to be willing to assume *full responsibility* not just for his *own* actions but also for the success or failure of our entire mission. If I asked someone to do something, and he told me, "That's not my job," I'd take a bite out of his ass, right then and there. *Everything* was *everybody's* job.

In addition, a guy had to be generous enough to give up all that he had—even his own life—for the other men on the mission. If you want to get all touchy-feely about it, you could call this quality "love." Whatever you call it, if you don't have it, you don't have character. The most unreliable man on any mission is the asshole who's self-obsessed. In a serious team effort, self-involvement is even more dangerous than stupidity or weakness.

Lastly, all of my guys had to have the right values. They had to be dedicated not only to their buddies but also to their country and their mission. If they weren't, they'd find it too easy to give up when things got ugly.

How do you find a man with character? You do it by analyzing the pattern of major decisions he's made during the course of his adulthood. Ask the guy about the toughest time in his life, and find out what he did to solve his problem. Did he wrestle with it until he whipped it, or did he just walk away and try something else? Has this guy taken care of other people—family, employees, or friends—or has he just taken care of himself? Can he tell you about some godawful, ballbusting tasks he's completed, or has he just been a nine-to-five guy? Has he been recognized for excellence, or has he just skated by? Has he ever righted a wrong and won the gratitude of others?

When you *do* find a man with character, bring him onto your team. Don't nitpick about his qualifications. Hire him over *better* qualified men with *less* character. A man with character can *learn* a job.

Don't be fooled by flamboyance, though. Often, people learn the *style* of character without gaining the substance of character. They swagger, make promises, and tell tales of their heroics, but they're just talking the talk. They don't *have* character—they *are* a character. They never walk the walk.

Sometimes, people start out having character but degenerate into someone who *is* a character. They'll win some battles and then get seduced by the spoils of victory. They'll fall in love with their own image and become parodies of themselves.

Here's something I learned about heroism, which is, essentially, character in action: There are times when you *feel* like a hero and times when you *are* a hero—but they're hardly ever the same time. When you're actually *being* heroic, you're usually too busy—or too scared—to *feel* heroic.

If a man is focused on his own reflection, he's probably lost sight of his mission.

In my opinion, a man who started out with character and then, unfortunately, *became* a character is Ross Perot. In the earlier part of his career, Perot focused the force of his considerable intelligence and will on building a powerful company, and then on rebuilding America. He had a vision and a plan. But when people started lionizing him, he apparently became infatuated with his own airbrushed, ad campaign image and started to believe his own PR. He seemed to think he'd suddenly become George Washington. When that happened, he was finished as a serious man.

Vanity is not the only destroyer of character, though. Character is also killed by laziness, dependence, and selfishness.

The collective character of the people in your company will form your organization's "corporate character." Often, a company will try to present the image of a positive corporate character to the public, but the presentation will be a sham, not reflective at all of the company's true character. If you want insight into a company's *real* character—as opposed to the company's avowed character—take a look at its major decisions over the past five or ten years.

Also, look at the minor decisions the company makes every day. They add up. Look at how the company treats the public and how it cares for its own people on a day-to-day basis. Even things like reserved parking spaces for bigwigs or executive bathrooms can indicate old-fashioned hierarchical rigidity. At SEAL Team Six, no one had "reserved" anything, and the commander pissed the same place as everyone else.

You can also ascertain an organization's true character by noting how it handles accountability and responsibility. At SEAL Team Six, accountability and responsibility were shared by each team member. Each member had to be willing to assume full responsibility not just for his own actions but also for the success or failure of the entire mission.

SEAL Team Six was what I call a "holographic organization." If you break a holographic image into many tiny pieces, you will see the entire image of the hologram in each of the pieces. Similarly, if you look at any one individual in a properly functioning team, you will see a reflection of the entire team and the entire mission.

Corporate consultant James Belasco often tells the story of an experience he had with the president of a $6 billion company. Belasco and the president were leaving the president's office one day when the president spotted a gardener raking leaves with a broken rake. The president asked the gardener why she was using the broken rake.

"Because that's what they gave me to use," she said.

He asked her why she didn't get a better one.

"That's not my job," she said.

As Belasco and the president walked on, the president got pissed off. His company was in trouble, and they couldn't even get someone to rake the leaves properly. Belasco asked the president who he blamed.

The president said he blamed the gardener's supervisor, who was supposed to supply the proper tools.

Belasco demurred.

The president took another shot at the problem. "If I'm going to be a hands-on leader, I guess *I'll* go get the rake."

"Whoa," said Belasco. "Is your getting the rake really going to fix the problem?"

The president asked Belasco who was to blame.

"The gardener," Belasco replied.

Belasco was dead right.

The gardener had the brains to solve the problem, had the time to solve the problem, and could doubtless have mustered the corporate backing to solve the problem. The gardener had the assets she needed to solve the problem, except for the one most important thing: character.

You *know* what Sun Tzu would have done with her.

As you've probably heard, before Benedict Arnold became infamous as an American traitor he was an exceptionally successful general in the Continental Army during the Revolutionary War. His victory at Bemis Heights, which led to the British surrender at Saratoga, has been called one of the most decisive battles in American history. But did you know what made Arnold turn traitor?

It wasn't because he was offered a position of great power in the British Army, or because he was offered a huge sum of money to defect, or because he became ideologically disenchanted with America.

What happened was, after Arnold's great series of victories, he expected a promotion. However, the members of the Continental Congress passed him over for promotion several times so that various congressmen could promote "favorite sons" from their own states.

This hurt Benedict Arnold's *feelings.*

He went into a snit and betrayed his country.

That was it. Whole story.

Arnold had every attribute of greatness, except for character. He couldn't stomach a little bit of humiliation, and it destroyed him.

Now, on a special wall in West Point, there hangs a collection of plaques bearing the names of the senior American officers of the Revolutionary War. In the most prominent position is George Washington's plaque. Near the rear hangs a plaque that says only "Major General." The date of birth on the plaque says "1741." But in the area where the name should be, there is just a chiseled-out blank space.

This is the plaque of Benedict Arnold, a man who could have been remembered as a great American—if only he'd realized the importance of character.

ROGUETOID: **Without the stability of character, you will not survive. Without the nobility of character, you *should* not survive.**

Lessons from War

The rising sun was orange and cold, like a harvest moon, as it broke the horizon just after dawn. My men and I were stumbling back to base camp in the orange light after an all-night river patrol. We were tired, hungry, and soaked with rain. We were looking forward to some hot coffee and a short nap. Then we saw the bodies, the blood, and the old woman weeping.

The old woman was the mother of a little Asian girl who had been helping us at our base area field hospital. The hospital was just a way station, a triage unit consisting of a few beds in a tent with a wood floor surrounded on the outside by four short walls made of sandbags. The girl, whose name was Mai Le, was gentle with the wounded men and always seemed to be smiling. What the hell she had to smile about, I don't know, but it always made me feel good to see her. Her mother always walked her to and from our camp. They were brave people.

In patchwork English, the mother told us that she, Mai Le, and two young men had been walking to the camp from their village, which was only two klicks up a trail, when they had been attacked by the local insurgents. The two young men, who were sprawled in front of us in odd, ungainly angles, had recently served with their national army but had come home to try to protect their village from insurgent infiltration.

"Where'd Mai Le go?" I asked the mother. "Where go?" She pointed up the trail toward the village.

"How long ago?" She gave me a blank look. I pointed at my wristwatch.

"Now," she said. "Minute."

I looked at my squad. None of them looked away,

6 1

except for one. His name was Ronald Newman. He was a skinny black kid from Pontiac, Michigan, and he was looking at the ground. "Sir," he murmured, "this ain't our fight. It ain't no never-mind to us."

"No," I said. "It's not." In fact, our rules of engagement expressly forbade us from becoming involved in "internal police issues," such as crimes against civilians, or disappearances. Standard operating procedure would be to report the "disturbance" to our CO, who'd relay the information to the village and provincial authorities. If everything went by the book, they might eventually come up with Mai Le's body—especially if the insurgents dumped it on the mother's doorstep, sufficiently disfigured to serve as a warning.

"Men, I'm goin' for a walk," I said. "Anybody wants to come, volunteer. If ya don't wanna go, no problem. Get back to camp and grab some sack."

I knew I wouldn't go alone. I knew my men. They had character. Dozens of times, the only thing that had kept my ass alive was what they had inside of them.

"I'm in," said Mickey Kalosh, my point man.

They all started to nod. But not Bonnie Ronnie Newman. Still looking at his feet, he said, "My enlistment's over in two *weeks*, man. I'm damn near *home*." A shooter near the end of his duty always hated any unnecessary risk. It was like double-daring God to shoot his ass off. Ronnie planned to return to CIVLANT in one piece.

"Don't sweat it," I said. I touched his shoulder. He looked away.

The rest of us double-timed down the trail.

Less than ten minutes later we saw her. She was tied to a tree, at a spot where the trail took a hard right. She had one rope around her midsection and another around her neck. Her face was going purple from lack of circulation, and even from a hundred yards away we could hear her breath coming in short, hard stabs.

"Looks like bear bait to me," I whispered. "Bet ya whoever tied her there is just off to either side, or both sides."

We split into two groups of three. Each group went forward, heading away from the trail at a forty-five-degree angle. When we got even with the girl, we'd cut straight in toward her and try to outflank the ambush.

We headed out, slipping silently through the under-growth. But before we could even cut back in, they opened up on us. We dove for the deck as bullets smashed down the vegetation around us.

Their firepower was overwhelming. We could barely raise our heads to shoot back.

I heard one of my men say, "We're fucked." The insurgents were moving closer. We were, indeed, fucked.

Then I heard the hollow whop of copter blades slapping the air, and the sound got louder in a hurry.

I saw the helicopter—not a big Army chopper but just a little HAL-3 Seawolf—diving toward the insurgent position like a bird of prey, with Mr. Ronald Newman hanging out the door and blazing away with a .50-caliber machine gun. Very dangerous stunt. Any insurgent with a forty-five could bring down one of those slow, piss-ant

Seawolves. Close-contact firefights were not the Seawolf's job.

As the Seawolf swooped level over the position, Ronnie leaned all the way out and dropped grenades with both hands. The damn things blew before they even hit the ground and almost knocked the Seawolf out of the air.

The insurgent position went silent. The survivors, if any, scuttled away into the jungle.

The chopper pilot put the Seawolf down in a small clearing, and I grabbed Mai Le and put her on board with Ronnie.

"You crazy son of a bitch," I said, "you get lonely?"

"Couldn't sleep. Too much noise."

The chopper lifted off, and we hurried the hell out of there.

A couple of years ago, me and a buddy from Southeast Asia were reminiscing at a reunion and he brought up Ronnie Newman.

"Wonder what the hell happened to him," he said. "You think he ever amounted to anything?"

"Ron Newman *always* amounted to something," I said. "What he had, you don't lose."

Lessons from Business, and from the Lives of Successful People

When you staff your team with people who have character, an extraordinary phenomenon occurs: Your team assumes a *collective character* that reinforces the character of every individual. If a team is put together carefully enough, it gains a character of its own that is clearly perceived by everyone who comes into contact with it. This happens with small teams, such as military platoons, and even large teams, like major corporations.

In the 1920s, when the Johnson & Johnson company was formed, its founder clearly defined its corporate character with the "J&J Credo." The credo said: "J&J's first responsibility is to our customers. J&J's second responsibility is to our employees. J&J's third responsibility is to our community. J&J's last responsibility is to our shareholders."

In our modern corporate culture, J&J's lack of emphasis on serving its shareholders is heretical. But over the long run, this philosophy has strengthened Johnson & Johnson by providing a consistent moral context for every major corporate decision.

Recently, the J&J Credo was put to its ultimate test when Tylenol, a J&J product, was tampered with, killing several people. The police in Chicago, where the incident occurred, advised the company's management not to withdraw Tylenol from the market nationwide because the tampering seemed to be confined to a limited area within Chicago.

The J&J management knew that a nationwide callback of Tylenol would cost about $350 million. But, for them, the choice was an easy one. Their corporate character, articulated by their credo, dictated nationwide removal of all Tylenol, to ensure the absolute safety of all the company's customers. Every bottle of Tylenol was removed from the shelves of every store in America, and the company went through an expensive and laborious process of designing tamperproof packaging, which soon became an industrial norm.

The J&J strategy proved to be extremely sound, commercially as well as morally. Reassured by the company's protectiveness, customers flocked back to Tylenol when it was reintroduced.

In retrospect, it appears as if J&J's display of character may have had national and international ramifications. When the incident occurred, at a time when terrorism was beginning to emerge worldwide, it was believed by most antiterrorist experts that terrorists—and even deranged loners—held the ability to incite widespread consumer panic virtually at will. Furthermore, many analysts believed that corporate greed and obsession with short-term profits would prevent the type of aggressive, expensive, private-sector counterattack that J&J launched.

However, when J&J showed a resolve that was equal to that of the Tylenol tamperer, it severely undercut the tactic.

J&J's response has become the standard. Now, virtually any product suspected of contamination is routinely recalled. Thus, not only is our world safer but it is also less vulnerable to disruption by terrorists and anyone else who decides to attack society.

An example of a company that showed a *lack* of character, in a somewhat similar test of moral fiber, is

Union Carbide. Shortly after the Tylenol incident, a leak from a Union Carbide plant in Bhopal, India, killed over three thousand people and caused permanent injury to tens of thousands more. Union Carbide provided only $1 million in emergency aid—a small sum for a major disaster—but the chairman of the company vowed that more help would soon be forthcoming. He pledged to spend the remainder of his career trying to make up for the damage. Within one year, though, he told a news magazine, "I overreacted." Instead of promising more help, he said, "I'm not going to play dead."

As a result of Union Carbide's intransigence, the courts took over. And the courts decided that Union Carbide had to pay $470 million in damages.

An excellent example of character in action is Mel Smith's school for disadvantaged kids, The Woodward Academy. Smith, who once helped run the federal Drug Enforcement Agency's Detroit office, recognized the futility of opposing the inner-city drug lifestyle without offering an alternative lifestyle. Therefore, he founded a school where poor kids could get hot meals, learn in peace and safety, and begin to take charge of their own futures. His vision was riddled with great financial risk, which several local institutions refused to share. But Smith, a man of steel strong character, forged ahead and took all the risks himself. His school has flourished and has rescued many lives.

The best way to instill corporate character in your company is to hire *individuals* with character, one by one. That's how Hewlett-Packard has built its world-class workforce.

When an individual interviews for a job at Hewlett-Packard—even an entry-level position—he or she faces a grueling round of interviews, some of which are conducted by high-ranking executives. The focus of interviews is not so much on technical skills as it is on character. Candidates are grilled primarily about intangible personal traits. For example, they might be asked to describe in detail a conflict they had with a friend, and how they resolved it.

Partly because of their emphasis on character, H-P has flourished in a high-tech industry that is too often dominated by techno-nerds with underdeveloped personalities. H-P's operational structure consists of small teams of people who work intensely on high-pressure projects, and the leaders of H-P are convinced that this structure works well only when everyone on the team has character.

One of the first great American industrialists to realize the importance of having people with character in his workforce was Henry Ford. Shortly after the turn of the century, the reigning attitude of the robber barons toward their workers was one of contempt. The working class was regarded as a herd of peasants who lacked not just the brains to better themselves but also the character. This attitude was a carryover from the aristocratic era, when character was believed to be largely a result of "breeding."

But Ford, a transcendentalist who believed in the perfectibility of the common man, sought out men of character to work in his plants and tried to instill character in those who lacked it.

Ford created a "Sociological Department" to serve as a moral watchdog over his men. The company's "social workers" went to each employee's home and requested to see the employee's marriage certificate, to make sure the employee wasn't living in sin, and asked to see the worker's account passbook, to make sure he was saving some money.

Often, Ford's social workers recommended that the worker study at night school or take a correspondence course.

The social workers also handed out Ford's "Rules of Living," which urged employees to use lots of soap and water at home, to not spit on the floor, to avoid buying things on the installment plan, and to resist sexual dalliances.

In return for meeting these demands, Ford instituted a profit-sharing plan that made wages so high that job seekers sometimes rioted outside his factory.

The net result of Ford's belief in the potential for character in every man was an unprecedented elevation of the working class. Ford's workers were peasants no longer. They were capitalists.

And what was the first thing these newly enfranchised men of character bought?

A car, of course.

ASK YOURSELF

- What were the three most important decisions you made during the last five years, and what do they say about your character?
- Is your company's corporate character consistent with your own personal character?
- When was the last time your executive team discussed your company's corporate character?

CHAPTER FOUR

TRAINING FOR VICTORY

"Above all, IBM's Thomas Watson trained, trained, trained."

—Peter Drucker, *Management*

"Winning is a habit."
—Vince Lombardi

In my most challenging week of training to become a U.S. Navy (Frogman) and now SEAL—a period aptly named Hell Week, which culminated on So Solly Day—I went through an exercise known as "demolitions exposure." This exercise was designed to familiarize us with not just the techniques of explosives detonation but also the *experience* of detonation.

In other words, they parked our asses next to a pile of explosives, then set it off.

From this, I learned that you can make *elaborate plans* about how to react in an explosion, but until that bomb goes off, *you don't know dick about it.*

Planning is not *training*.

Training is training. And training is an area that most companies, and most people, are deficient in. A recent survey showed that only 70 percent of American companies train their executives, and only about 25 percent train their production forces and salespeople. Furthermore, for every dollar the federal government pays for private training programs, it contributes $3,200 for buildings and technology.

But putting buildings before brains is stupid.

Even before he became secretary of labor, Robert Reich recognized that of all of America's business assets, the only one that isn't "portable" is our workforce. Virtually everything else in our country can be picked up and packed off. But our people *stay*. The same principle probably applies to your own company.

Much of America's current jeopardy in the business world stems from its neglect of training. It's widely believed that the top 10 percent of our workforce stacks up favorably with that of any other nation in the world. But after our elite 10 percent, our quality of personnel drops off drastically. Almost one in five Americans is functionally illiterate, and this speaks volumes about the failure of America to educate its workers.

Ross Perot once noted that "brains and wits will beat capital spending ten times out of ten." As technology continues to burgeon, this is becoming increasingly true.

In today's complex business environment, it's absurd

to try to grow any company, or to implement any strategy, without strenuous training and testing programs. Your vision, your plans, and your follow-through will go straight to hell if your workforce has its head up its ass.

Unfortunately, a lot of hotshot executives think that if their plan is good enough, their employees should be able to *just do it.* However, in the words of the dedicated and courageous American runner Mary Slaney—who's never won an Olympic medal—"If you could just *do* it, I'd have done it by now."

I'll give you an example of an arrogant organization that set a lofty goal, made grand plans, and then expected its workers to just do it. This organization switched from a long-standing system of arduous training and testing to a management format called Success Oriented Management. The new management system, installed in the early 1980s, called for setting goals that were based upon the capabilities and possibilities of *technology,* rather than people. It was assumed that technology could solve virtually any problem that developed and that the people involved could find a way to keep pace.

This system caused many people at the organization to mistake *prediction* for *reality* and to assume that things were running more smoothly than they really were.

At the time, one skeptic characterized the system as follows: "It means you design everything to cost, then pray."

As the organization's primary project progressed, the project was characterized by evasion of difficult problems, constant redesigning of hardware, endless schedule adjustments, and dangerous accidents. Instead of training workers to achieve excellence—and to demand excellent support systems from their managers—the organization tried to high-tech its way past every obstacle. The approach didn't work, the schedule went way offtrack, and pressure for results increased.

The organization was NASA. The project was the space shuttle.

The net result was the 1986 explosion of the *Challenger.*

When the *Challenger* blew, one of the victims was Christa McAuliffe, who was to have been the first civilian in space. Putting her aboard had been nothing more than a publicity stunt, intended to get NASA more press—and thus more funding. At about the same time, NASA had also sponsored a bullshit "Pepsi challenge," to determine whether astronauts would drink more Pepsi than Coke on their mission. This, too, had been a blatant publicity stunt. In fact, the entire group of space shuttle contractors who *built* the machine—with the job going to the lowest bidder—had been gradually trained to think more like timing-obsessed publicists than like engineers. That was *ignorant.* People have to be trained for *exactly* what they really do.

For example, the training of the Federal Express workforce focuses strongly on the single, primary vision that created the company in the first place: *overnight delivery.* FedEx has trained its workers to ship and track packages so efficiently that the U.S. Army, in designing its supply system for the Gulf War, copied the training techniques of FedEx.

It's also important not just to train your people for the central job that they *do,* but also to train them for the job they're doing *now: this* year, *this* month, *today.* One of the criticisms of the military, which is often extrapolated to the business world, is that generals tend to train their forces to fight the last war instead of the next one. A recent example of this occurred during Operation Desert Storm. When General Norman Schwarzkopf was preparing his ground assault against Iraq, he realized that the Iraqis were training their soldiers to fight against vast human-wave assaults, like the ones the Iranians had used against Iraq in the Iraq-Iran war. The Iraqis were placing their tanks behind revetments, laying out barbed wire, and building elaborate minefields. When Schwarzkopf's highly mobile troops swept *around* these stationary fortifications, the Iraqis didn't know whether to shit or go blind.

In contrast, the U.S. Marine Corps is now actively training its men for the *next* war. The Marine Corps is currently engaged in an ambitious redesign of its most basic tactics and function. The radical new redesign, called Operation Sea Dragon, places unprecedented emphasis on communications and on information technology.

Let me tell you something else about training. This is something that a lot of smart people don't seem to know: It's just as important to train your *"unimportant"* people as your *"important"* people. For one thing, there are a hell of a lot more of them, and they're the foundation of your organization.

For another, you desperately need some of these "little guys" to grow into "big guys." If you don't raise people through the ranks—and instead hire your top people from the outside—you'll create a company in which the top layer of execs is out of touch with the nuts-and-bolts operation of your company.

At the Hollywood talent agencies, which have practically taken over the entertainment industry, *everybody* starts as a "little guy," serving as a secretary and assistant to a full-fledged agent. This type of "full-dress battle training" is unbeatable. It throws neophytes into the real world, in real time, and lets them hone their skills in actual operations. If they don't have the brains or the guts to hack it, they find out right away—and so does their boss.

You should insist on this type of realism in *all* your training. Don't play schoolmarm with your trainees; toss their butts into the real deal, and see who sinks and who swims. Even the training of top execs should be more like a dress rehearsal than a day in school. If you're training people to do research on a competitor, give them a quick briefing, then boot them onto the street.

Here's what can happen when you sacrifice realism in

training. A few years ago in California, a police officer got killed in a shootout while trying to reload his gun. He couldn't reload *quickly* enough because his hands were full of empty shells. As he'd been shooting, he'd been picking up his shells. He'd been *trained* at the police firing range *always* to pick up his shells as he shot. Why? It kept the range clean.

When you finish training people, train them *again*. Training is not a one-shot deal; it must be continuous. No one is smart enough to learn everything in one session. Besides, things change as time passes, so your training should be constantly updated.

Similarly, if you have a vision of a new product, and a plan to market it, test the *shit* out of it before you commit your company's resources to it. Make sure it *works*, and make sure people *like* it. Don't try to perfect it in the lab, because you're not going to sell it to laboratory technicians. Take it out to the real world to see if it will sink or swim. This approach will, among other things, shorten the development cycle of your product.

You've got to test your people *and* your products, in difficult conditions, to see if they'll "break." If they do, you'll find out what their weaknesses are. Then you can either fix the weakness or shitcan the product or the person—*before* they do any serious damage to your company.

General Colin Powell believes in training troops in conditions that are as close as possible to actual combat. While preparing his men to fight in the Korean War, the young Colin Powell began training his troops all night and making them sleep during the day, reasoning that "North Korea wouldn't be fighting us nine-to-five."

Near the end of their training, Powell accompanied his men on an ugly, all-night mountain hike that ended ten miles from camp. As the men collapsed at their destination, Powell ordered them up—so they could hike back over the mountains to camp.

They hit camp at dawn, singing cadence as they marched in flawless formation past the general's quarters.

Powell now remembers this training episode vividly— equally as well as he remembers great victories in battle—as "magical, one of the treasured memories of my life."

If your training is intense enough, you'll remember it always.

After all, that's the *point* of it, right?

ROGUETOID: Training should be so realistic that it makes real missions feel fake.

Lessons from War

One of my shooters slumped next to me as I sat on a dirt floor in the dust-darkened bowels of a Navy training facility at Eglin Air Force Base. We were training to rescue the American hostages in Iran.

Shortly before, in November of 1979, Iranian militants

had taken over the U.S. embassy and had captured its staff. Eight days later, we'd formed the hostage rescue unit that would soon spawn SEAL Team Six, my elite squad of counterterrorist warriors.

The shooter who was sprawled next to me was so soaked with sweat that the dust from the training facility was glued to him like a chocolate shell.

"Commander," he said in a fatigue-slurred voice, between gulps of air, "am I gonna *make* it?" He knew that a lot of the men here—all tested fighters—were going to wash out.

"Hell if I know," I said.

He had a big set of eyes on him, almond shaped and brown, and he fixed them on me plaintively. "Shit," I said, "you'll make it. Just catch your fucking *breath,* so's you don't *die* on me."

If some other guy had asked me that, I might've busted his balls, to motivate him. But this kid, Ron Choi, from Hawaii, got better motivation from a little kindness, so that's how I treated him.

Choi jumped back up before he could pull in even one decent breath. "Thank you, sir!" he said. He charged back into the exercise. Choi was a softhearted kid, but he was a tiger.

All seventy-six of the men in my command were practicing close-quarter battle, or CQB, in preparation for man-to-man fighting in an urban environment. These men were all prepared to hit the streets of Tehran as part of a small, special warfare unit and to engage a force that might be inordinately larger. The only advantages we held were in planning, character, weaponry, and training.

All the men at this facility knew the consequences of capture, and they were all prepared for this to be their final mission, if necessary.

And they were even *more* prepared to kick some Ayatollah *ass.*

On this day, we were practicing storming the type of "safe house" where the hostages probably were being held. One segment of our rescue team had already deployed operatives in Iran, who'd been tasked with locating the hostages. Two of them were SEAL buddies of mine. After the successful completion of their sneak-and-peek mission, the rest would be up to us.

My men were practicing hitting a house in two-man teams. We'd already worked our way, in incremental steps, from assaults with dry fire, to assaults with live fire, and from assaults with .357 Magnum revolvers to assaults with 9mm pistols. The Magnum "wheel guns" were possibly more efficient for this mission, but they would have been identified immediately as American guns, in the event of capture. Besides, the automatic pistols had more bullets in their magazines. An important part of our training was testing weapons, to see what worked well and what didn't. As I've mentioned, we were a walking, talking R&D department.

When the last two-man team finished the drill, I gathered everyone around. "Listen up, girls," I said. "Things are going to get a little hairier now. We're gonna hit doors in four-man teams, with live ammo. It's gonna be more congested and more chaotic. Just like Tehran. As you mass outside the door, stay close enough to touch each other. Then, first man through the door goes left, next man right, then left, then right. As you go in, hug the walls and throw shit toward the middle of the room— lamps, chairs, whatever. That'll help put something between you and the enemy. When you clear one room, sweep to the next, but don't forget closets. Don't lose your rhythm as a team, and if one of the 'enemy' gets you with his wax bullets, for Chrissake, don't kill the guy. Remember, people, *live ammo*. Fingers off triggers! Fingers off triggers! Questions?" Nobody said anything.

Everybody was tense. That was good. This had to be painful and scary. If it wasn't, we were just playing wooden soldiers, and we'd soon pay the price. The more you sweat in training, the less you bleed in combat.

All these men had already gone through the brutal induction program for SEALs, but my training was even nastier than that had been. These guys had already gone up to a week at a time without sleep, and they'd been tested physically and mentally. They'd endured severe harassment and torturous physical tests. But after a few weeks with me, climbing oil rigs, free-falling at night through low-oxygen altitudes, and getting their skin cut apart with wax bullets, they were getting *nostalgic* about their induction training.

"First team!" I yelled. "Go!"

They kicked the door and stormed inside, keeping their backs to the walls and heaving furniture toward

8 1

the middle of the room. They executed the maneuver well.

"Next!"

Four more guys positioned outside the door, then they smashed through it and poured into the room. Suddenly: *BOOM!*

As the dust still swirled, a man lay twitching on the floor. "Corpsman! *Now!*" I yelled, and three or four men ran off for medical assistance. I knelt over the wounded man and pushed hard where the blood was pumping out of him.

In a shaky voice, somebody said, "Sir, I tripped, and my gun went off."

"Fingers *off* triggers," I said. As if it mattered now.

The wounded man gazed up at me. I looked into the big fucking Bambi eyes of Ron Choi. He was gravely wounded. His face was going white under the dust. "Am I gonna make it?" he whispered.

"Quit fuckin' asking me that," I said quietly. "I *told* you you're in." He managed to smile. At least, part of his face did.

After we loaded Ron on a medevac helicopter, we took a short break, talked about what had gone wrong, and went back to work.

The man who shot Ron was quickly isolated and then separated from the unit.

Ron died a few days later. The best we could do for him was to fly in his wife and his mom at the end.

Hell of it is, we never did make it to Tehran. White House decision. But we made it plenty of other places, and I can flat-ass guarantee you nobody ever made that same mistake again.

And wherever we went, Ron Choi was with us—at least in our heads—telling us to be goddamn careful, and to train, train, train, and to remember every damn thing we'd ever been taught.

Lessons from Business, and from the Lives of Successful People

In January of 1945, Thomas Watson Jr., the son of the founder of IBM, went to work at his father's company.

When he arrived at his father's office that morning, Tom Watson Jr. was escorted down the hall by his dad to the office of a tough, ballbreaking, midlevel executive. "Tom," said the father, "you've met Charlie Kirk. You're going to be his assistant."

Tom Watson Jr. was stunned. He'd had something a little more elegant in mind, like . . . Vice President in Charge of Waiting for Dad to Retire.

Instead, he was ordered to sit in a hard chair at the side of Charlie Kirk's desk, and to watch and learn. If Kirk needed coffee, Watson fetched it. If Kirk stayed late, Watson stayed late.

But Watson got a hell of an education from Kirk, and eventually became president of the company. In fact, Tom Watson Jr. retooled IBM for the postwar economy and made IBM far more successful than even his father had.

One element of his father's business that Watson never changed, though, was its emphasis on training. More than any other large corporation in America, IBM has emphasized training as the most important element in its corporate culture.

For example, one recent IBM advertisement focused on a worker who had gone through a half-dozen major retraining periods in a twenty-five-year career in order to keep pace with changing technology. The message was: At IBM, we stay a step ahead of you.

As long ago as the 1920s, IBM introduced the concept of training women for service jobs, and the company *still* has the best sales training program of any of America's technology companies.

After every promotion, an IBM employee must take a complete training course, and everyone in the company is required to spend the equivalent of one full workweek every year in retraining classes. In just the area of quality control alone, more than 150,000 IBM employees were trained over one five-year period.

In the 1980s, with the emergence of the personal computer industry, IBM appeared to be in jeopardy of losing its position as America's premiere high-tech hardware company. However, IBM's emphasis on training and retraining—which had kept the company's workforce current on virtually all technical issues—allowed the massive company to adjust to the changing marketplace. Now, IBM is as dominant in personal computers as it once had been in mainframes.

Many Japanese and German companies are just as

zealous as IBM about training. Many analysts think this is the major reason Japan and Germany have kicked America's ass at automaking. One example of this is the Japanese carmaker Nissan. When Nissan opened its plant in Tennessee, it spent $63 million on training in that one factory alone—more than $30,000 per employee. A great deal of this training took place not in classrooms but on the floor of the new factory and involved solving real problems in real time as the assembly line howled.

Good training doesn't always have to be done on a regimented, formal basis, though. At Hewlett-Packard, there is a long-standing tradition of employees leaving their product-design projects on the top of their desks. It's understood that any engineer walking by is free to take a look at the project, in order to learn about it—and, hopefully, to contribute to it.

At Nordstrom, the department store chain that's famous for its customer service, executives run a seat-of-the-pants training program by consistently "overstaffing" areas of the sales floor with both managers and salespeople. Doing this allows salespeople to learn from managers, and managers to learn from salespeople. This format also serves as an informal grooming method for new Nordstrom managers, who often rise from the ranks of salespeople.

McDonald's is another company that emphasizes training its ground-level troops. The hamburger chain practically invented the fast-food market by training teenagers to work with precision and self-responsibility.

If you're a manager, you should never kid yourself into thinking that it's the white-collar guys who are the backbone of your organization. They may be the brains of the outfit, but the blue-collar people are the heart and soul.

McDonald's founder, Ray Kroc, believed so much in the importance of training blue-collar workers that he generally refused to donate money to higher education. Kroc once said, "I have been wooed by some of the finest educational institutions in the land, but I tell them they will not get a cent from me unless they put in a trade school."

Most well-run companies are as diligent about *testing their products* as they are about training their workforce. Their managers recognize that product testing is an integral part of the early phase of any project. Just as I refused to send my men on missions with substandard equipment, these managers refuse to send their sales and marketing people onto the streets with poor products to push through the pipeline.

Procter & Gamble is considered by some observers to have a "testing fetish." One competitor said that "P&G tests and tests and tests. You can see them coming for months, often years. But you know that when they get there, it is probably time for you to move to another niche."

A good testing procedure, however, doesn't have to be done by the book. It can often be just as effective if it's done rogue-style.

Here's an example. A few decades ago, the manager of

a struggling camera company was walking through his factory when he saw an engineer working with a huge, adjustable, close-up lens.

Intrigued, he asked the engineer what it would cost to outfit a consumer-oriented camera with the lens.

"A fortune," the engineer said.

"How much for just one prototype?" the manager asked.

The reply: "A *small* fortune."

The manager asked the engineer to manufacture a prototype. When it was finished, the manager took the camera home and showed it to his guests at a dinner party. They all looked through the lens, fiddled with it, and were blown away. The phrase "high tech" wasn't even in use yet, but, by God, this was *it*. Everyone at the party wanted to buy one. It would cost far more than a regular camera—but what the hell! It was amazing!

The lens was a zoom lens.

The camera company was Bell & Howell.

The manager got rich—the Rogue Warrior way. He had a vision, he took a risk, he broke the rules, he did his testing—and he won the game.

We're now at the end of our preparation phase. We've run through the sequence of creating a vision, setting goals, formulating a plan, dictating the rules of engagement, building a high-character team to implement the vision, and training that team to win.

Now it's time for the action phase.

Hang on!

ASK YOURSELF

- How many things have you learned on the job that could have been taught earlier?
- Are your company's training exercises realistic? How close do they come to the real thing?
- Do people sometimes quit your company because of the difficulty of your training programs? If not, why not?

PART 3

OPERATIONAL SUCCESS— THE ROGUE WARRIOR WAY

CHAPTER FIVE

Mistake Is NOT a Dirty Word

"When there is fear of failure, there will be failure."
—General George Patton

"Don't be afraid of failure. Be more afraid of not trying."
—General Colin Powell

"Success can only be achieved through repeated failure and introspection."
—Soichiro Honda, Founder, Honda Motors

You know who was the biggest fuck-up ever to lead this country? Abraham Lincoln. Without a doubt.

Lincoln made more mistakes than any president before or since.

He was also arguably our greatest president.

Contradiction? Nope. Just simple logic. Lincoln *achieved* more because he *tried* more. And because he tried more, he failed more.

Runner-up for Most Mistakes in the White House goes to Franklin Roosevelt. Same logic. When FDR took over, the country was in a shambles after the do-nothing administration of Herbert Hoover. So Roosevelt was forced to implement his motto, "Above all, *try* something." During his epic first hundred days, he launched his controversial "alphabet soup" attack: WPA, CCC, SEC, etc. Some of these social programs turned into nothing more than glorious goatfucks. But others worked and saved the country from utter disaster.

However, during the unprecedented economic boom since the end of World War II, far too many American political leaders and business managers have gotten soft, satisfied, and afraid to be bold. They won't do anything that might taint their own résumés or piss off their constituencies or boards of directors. After all, life is good now—why rock the boat?

But prosperity isn't the only factor that has contributed to the psychological castration of our current crop of leaders and managers. Two other major postwar trends have also exacerbated the modern epidemic of timidity.

One is the ascendance of technology, which has elevated science to the status of a religion. These days, many managers seem to think that business itself is a science, and that all business problems can be worked out in the "test tube" of statistical modeling and market research. That's bullshit. Business revolves around *people*—customers and workers—and anything that's based on people is ultimately *unpredictable*. If you *really* want to know if something will work, at some point you've got to stop testing, grab your balls, and take the plunge into the real world marketplace.

The other big trend that is killing boldness—and, with it, the trial-and-error approach—is institutionalism. These days, *everything* is an institution: business, labor, education, medicine, law, the military, and *God knows*, government. Each institution has so many rules, regulations, customs, and conventions that there's no room left for somebody to say, "Hell, let's *try* something—it might *work!*" Instead, every idea has to work its way through the research committee, the budget committee, the executive committee, and the committee for redundancy committee.

If you think America today is as experimental and freewheeling as America used to be, take a look at our latest generation, the so-called Gen-X. I hate to sound like an old, "kids-today" fart, but these people are *sheep*. Their idea of rebellion is to *smoke cigars*. To them, risk means not using sunscreen.

Far too many of today's young people are simply *afraid to fail*, but this fear of failure will ultimately *cause* their failure. Too many people today have no guts, and they'll get no glory.

Don't get me wrong. I'm not saying you should rush into battle half-cocked. I've spent half this book telling you how to prepare for a fight. But once you've reached the operational phase of your project, you've got to put your fears aside and go for the gusto. George Patton put it like this: "The time to take counsel of your fears is before you make an important battle decision. That's the time to listen to every fear you can imagine. When you have collected all of the facts and fears and made your decision, turn off all your fears and go ahead! Any man who is afraid of failure will never win! Any man who is afraid to die will never really live!"

If you're afraid to make mistakes, it will be almost impossible for you to succeed, because you will be unable to *learn*. You won't be able to find out what works and what doesn't. Mistakes are messengers, telling us that we have not yet fully understood the situation. Every mistake is an opportunity to correct the course of action.

In science, the scientific method consists of subjecting a theory to a series of experiments. If a theory doesn't work the first time, it's modified and tested again. The scientist who modifies his theory is not considered to be a failure.

Similarly, in shooting a gun, the shooter sights in on the target, takes a shot, measures his miss, and then adjusts his sights. The shooter who adjusts his sights is *not* condemned as a failure.

To achieve any kind of progress, in business or in life, you've got to *try* something, see how well it works, fix whatever doesn't work, and then try again. This process is what Soichiro Honda, the founder of Honda Motors, calls "failure and introspection." Another phrase for it, cited in the classic business book *Thriving on Chaos*, is "failing forward."

General Charles Krulak, commandant of the U.S. Marine Corps, is now employing the "failing forward" process as he redesigns the Marine Corps for the future. During this redesign phase, Krulak said recently he is "giving the Marines freedom to fail." Krulak believes that any successful evolutionary process is bound to be riddled with mistakes. His goal is to see that these mistakes illuminate the Corps' true needs and are systematically corrected as the new Corps emerges.

To get maximum benefit from the trial-and-error method, though, you've got to apply it *correctly*. First of all, you've got to *recognize* when you've made a mistake. Don't put good money after bad. Then you've got to *learn* from your mistake and make adjustments. If you're in business, you've got to learn *fast* and react fast; you can't dick around while your *competition* learns from your mistake. Furthermore, you've got to resist getting caught up in finger-pointing, guilt, and fear. That bullshit is appropriate for children, not managers. If you indulge in it, you'll probably make the same mistakes again and again. If this becomes a pattern, it means that you're not yet ready to lead.

In short: Try. Learn. Try again. Don't expect perfection. Don't punish scapegoats. Move on.

That's what Abraham Lincoln did when he grappled with his most gut-churning problem: finding a general who could win the Civil War.

When the war began, Lincoln went with General Winfield Scott, who was the most experienced man available. But that was a colossal fuck-up, because Scott, at age seventy-five, was too old and tired for the job. So Lincoln turned to a younger man, General Irvin McDowell. Another big mistake. McDowell was *too* young for the job and was intimidated by it. Lincoln then looked to General George McClellan to provide a steady hand. McClellan was an improvement, but he was so "steady" that he was damn near comatose, and did virtually nothing. Next: General Henry Halleck. He wasn't afraid to attack, but he got whipped so badly it shattered his nerves. Finally, after four more "auditions," Lincoln settled on Ulysses S. Grant and found, to his delight, that "Grant fights!" After Grant took over, the war ended in thirteen months.

Every time Lincoln fired a general, though, he let the general down easy, kicking him upstairs or making him a figurehead. In doing so, Lincoln maintained the army's morale and didn't create enemies.

But privately, Lincoln admitted his mistakes, cut his losses, learned his lessons, reacted swiftly, didn't make the same mistakes twice—and won the war.

Learn from Lincoln. Be bold. Try something. Watch it turn to shit. Then try, try again.

ROGUETOID: **Yesterday's solutions are today's mistakes, and today's mistakes are tomorrow's innovations.**

Lessons from War

It was the eve of a national holiday in Southeast Asia, so I assumed things would be quiet for a few days. That was my first mistake.

An unwritten rule of engagement in this conflict said that when the enemy took a break, we should, too. I thought it was a bullshit rule, though, and wanted to cook up some action. So I organized an excursion into enemy territory, up near the Burmese border—or, to be more precise, maybe just a little bit *across* the Burmese border. That was against the *written* rules of engagement, but fuck that. The enemy had tens of *thousands* of troops across the border, shuttling in supplies.

We deployed from the provincial capital of Chiang Luan, where we were stationed. Just before we left, I filed a "fire plan" with the provincial commanding officer, detailing where we were going. The CO was a certain Colonel Numbnuts, who'd long ago traded his taste for war for a taste for cheap whiskey. Theoretically, if the colonel knew our coordinates, he would be able to rise from his stupor and call in artillery support for us if we needed it. But, in the real world, you don't call in artillery for a dozen SEALs hiding in the jungle, as if they were Patton's Second Armored Division. Furthermore, I didn't want to tell *anybody* where we were going, not even our own support staff, because in this Third World action, there were too many conflicted interests. Colonel Numbnuts might reveal our fire plan to his counterpart in the intelligence office, who might mention it to his locally hired secretary, who might discuss it with her cousin, who might happen to be out in the bush carrying a Chinese-built rifle.

Nonetheless, I was under a great deal of pressure to file the plan, so I did. But I lived to regret it.

We whipped up the Manoc River in our PBR (patrol boat, river) and slid into the water about eight klicks upriver. We were farther up the Manoc than any PBR had ever been.

My goal was to intercept the enemy as they crossed the Burmese border with supplies, and to wish them a happy holiday with a fireworks show.

But shortly after we crawled out of the water, the shit began to hit the fan. As we were moving across a rice field in single file, my point man froze and raised his hand for us to halt. He looked back at me with saucer eyes and pointed at a tiny button protruding from the muck. "Minefield," I whispered to the men. Shit! I'd walked my men into an acre of noisemakers and ball-breakers. Technically, I guess you could say that was a mistake, too, if you want to jump all over my ass.

I took over point and led the men through the mine-field. It took us two hours to cover four hundred feet.

Then, for no reason but instinct—which, in Southeast Asia, was the best reason of all to do something—I suddenly stopped and dropped. As I fell, I felt the whoosh of an AK-47 round slam past my head. The night lit with fire, and the silence exploded. The jungle was thick with shadowy figures.

"Jesus, boss, there's a good *fifty* of 'em!" somebody yelled.

We'd been ambushed. And not by some piss-ant patrol. This was a major force. They *had* to have known we were coming.

I vowed never again to fully reveal my plans to anyone I didn't trust completely.

We held them off, radioed the PBR, and hauled ass. On the way back through the minefield—running so fast we hardly hit the ground—I was glad that we already knew a path that was at least half-ass safe.

As we jumped on the PBR, I heard one of the mines explode. Tough luck, papa-san.

We roared off, and I radioed HQ. While I was on the radio, our PBR took more fire. The hills were alive with the sound of gunfire, and the enemy appeared to be moving toward Chiang Luan.

Base camp told me they were under attack, too. I told them more trouble was on the way. They were grateful for the info, which made me feel better. It helped to know that some good had come from our mission.

The minute we hit town, a Special Forces major told me about a new crisis. Two American schoolteachers were trapped in a building several blocks away.

"We'll go get 'em," I said.

"Negative! Nobody leaves! Colonel's orders."

I picked the son of a bitch up by his lapels and lifted him off the ground. "Say again?" I said. "My ears are all fucked up from the firefight."

"Oh, go get 'em," he whined, "but tell the colonel where you're going."

"Absolutely, sir." Well, piss on that. I'd *learned* from my misfortune.

We rushed onto the streets still wearing our bush-camouflage. Big mistake. In the barren, concrete city, we stuck out like Christmas trees.

We went building to building and roof to roof, just like in an old World War II movie.

When we got to the building where the American women were, my men ran in to get them as I stood sentinel outside. Suddenly there was a commotion from around the corner, and I dived for the nearest cover, a scroungy little bush. A squad of enemy zipped past as I scrunched behind the bush amongst an assortment of dog turds. They didn't see me, partly because of the dark, and mostly because the last thing they were looking for was a round-eye in jungle garb. One thing I'd learned is that when you make a mistake that puts you in a unique, unexpected position, you can often find a way to use it to your advantage.

By the time we got the women back to headquarters, the fighting was already beginning to slack off.

As the enemy withdrew from Chiang Luan, I led a squad of men out to see if we could pick off stragglers.

By daylight, we were out in the countryside, hunkered

down in a graveyard behind headstones, when I saw a company of about ninety enemy heading past. We ambushed them. I expected them to scatter. But these bastards dropped to their knees, returned fire, and began executing a complex flanking maneuver.

Damn! Another mistake. But mistakes are the currency of warfare, because warfare consists of nothing but taking one calculated risk after another.

Their counterattack didn't fall apart until we hit them with a variable-time fused artillery, a detonation device that explodes in midair. When we laid the VT in their laps, and over our own position, they broke contact and retreated. When they left, we had all of forty-eight bullets left.

Conventional wisdom says, after that kind of encounter, extract and get back to camp ASAP—especially if you're out of ammo. But I kept us out all day and all night. I could *smell* an ambush coming. The force we'd fought was just too smart to let us off the hook. They'd executed their maneuvers as if they'd just gotten done reading General Carl von Clausewitz's classic, *On War*.

Some of the guys bitched about the campout, but so what? My job was to lead, not *be* led.

When we finally got back, we found out that the people who'd come down the road just ahead of us had gotten blown to hell by a booby trap. If we'd come back the night before, it would have been us.

As we settled down with a few gallons of beer, some of my men—including the guys who'd been bitching—

came around to give me a cheerful fuck-you-very-much for getting us back. Soldiers don't have to do that, but my men were more than soldiers. They were warriors.

God knows, I was making mistakes. But every one of them was making me a better leader.

Lessons from Business, and from the Lives of Successful People

When a young mechanic named Henry Ford decided to go into the auto business in 1899, the industry was already in full swing. Ford certainly did not invent the automobile, because there were already about four thousand of them on the road. But Ford was able to raise $15,000 from a few key investors and soon had a prototype that went about twenty-five miles per hour.

Ford was maniacal about precision, and to ensure quality he insisted that each of his cars be essentially handmade. However, his backers grew impatient with his insistence on perfection. After all, they were in business to make a profit, and Ford's approach appeared to be doomed. Ford resisted their suggestions, which was clearly a mistake; they pulled out, and his company folded.

Ford, who was a trial-and-error mechanic, rather than an engineer, was undaunted. He had a great deal of character. He remarked that "You've got to keep going and keep doing."

To gain publicity, Ford built a race car that went

almost sixty miles per hour and hired famous driver Barney Oldfield to race it. Ford soon attracted new partners. By this time, though, there were thirty-eight car companies in existence. Most were in New England, which was the center of the industry, although a few, including Ford, were in Michigan.

Because the cars made by Ford's new company were built so painstakingly, they were expensive, costing about $35,000 in today's dollars.

Again, Ford was pressured by his moneymen, who demanded that he stage an event that would show the world how *good* the expensive Ford cars were. So Ford himself hurtled one of his cars across a frozen lake and set the world's record for speed. But the high-speed run had been absurdly dangerous, and Ford emerged from the car pale and shaking.

The risk paid off, though. News of Ford's death-defying stunt traveled around the world, and interest in his cars surged. But just as quickly, interest died when people found out how costly the cars were.

Ford realized he'd made a terrible mistake. He had designed an excellent car but had tooled it so precisely that no one could afford it.

Ford went back to work. Because he had created a seemingly insoluble problem for himself, he searched for radical solutions. Finally, he came up with a new process for constructing cars. Instead of having several mechanics grouped around one car, he rotated each car from one assemblage station to another.

Ford thought this was a good idea, which would make

his new car, the Model T, affordable. He thought the construction process might even someday change how other products were manufactured.

He called his process the "assembly line."

In less than two years, Henry Ford was one of the richest young men in America.

About sixty years after the introduction of the assembly line, a new wave of entrepreneurs brought the assembly line process to the restaurant business and created the fast-food industry. One of these entrepreneurs was Dave Thomas, the founder of Wendy's. Like most entrepreneurs—who typically pioneer in uncharted territories—Thomas excels at the trial-and-error approach.

Because he's bold, Thomas is not afraid to make mistakes. In fact, Thomas says that "Mistakes make the man."

Thomas made three major mistakes that could have ruined his career. But he learned from each mistake, reacted appropriately, and emerged more successful than ever.

His first major mistake, he says, was dropping out of high school. His lack of education, he believes, was "an awful disadvantage in the business world."

However, Thomas discovered soon after he quit school that "dropouts have to work harder just to get by, and they have to work super hard to break through." Thomas forced himself to work exceptionally hard, and it paid off. Later, long after he'd become a multimillionaire, he returned to his high school studies and earned a high school equivalency degree.

The second mistake Thomas made was to fail to make plans for the future after Wendy's had become a successful local business. Instead of planning for more growth, Thomas rested on his laurels—and it almost lost him the opportunity to expand Wendy's into a national chain.

But when Thomas discovered how much damage had been done by his lack of planning, he became obsessive about planning. He learned to make plans not only for how to succeed but also for how to react to failures. "Now," he says, "I snoop around for problems, to turn them into growth opportunities."

Thomas made his third big mistake soon after Wendy's became a national success and was listed on the New York Stock Exchange. When this happened, Thomas built a glamorous and huge corporate headquarters and filled the building with a glut of new executives. He soon found, though, that his staff was too large to efficiently solve the types of problems his company faced.

He responded by cutting back on staff and allowing the staff to continue to shrink, in proportion to the growth of the chain.

From these three major mistakes, Dave Thomas learned that "mistakes are deadly only if you don't follow up on them, and change your way of living."

You don't always have to change your course of action, though, in order to benefit from a mistake. Sometimes, through perseverance and creativity, you can make the best of a bad decision and gain benefits from it that you would have missed if you'd done the "right" thing. A master of this approach is Bill Gates, the legendary head of Microsoft.

Gates applied this approach during the long, painful development of his most monumentally important products.

In the early 1980s, Gates had a vision that he believed might change his industry. Gates wanted to make IBM and IBM-clone computers easier to use, so he launched research into a computer program that would keep IBM users from having to type in long codes. Instead, they would just "point" at on-screen pictures. He called the program Windows.

Gates put thirty of his best programmers on the job, but it was a *bear*. Before Windows was done, it would consume eighty work years of labor.

After several years of work, though, which created considerable anticipation in the industry, Windows still wasn't working the way Gates wanted.

Previously, Gates's basic strategy had been to launch programs before they were perfect, and work out the bugs later. But he refused to do this with Windows because he'd allowed himself to become emotionally attached to the project. He wanted it to be flawless. As a business tactic, though, this was a mistake. It frustrated the companies that worked with Microsoft and made them doubt the young company's capabilities.

In early 1985, two of Microsoft's staunchest allies, computer makers Tandy and Compaq, released new models that were *supposed* to be equipped with Windows. But they weren't because Gates didn't think Windows was fast enough yet. Thus, Gates lost his chance to piggyback the introduction of Windows onto his allies' introductions of their new products. Within the industry, this was regarded as a major gaffe. It meant that Gates would have to sell Windows by itself on retail shelves, which would be much harder.

Gates then made another mistake. He pushed his engineers to rush their schedules—and their schedules were already ridiculously unrealistic. As a result, a sense of crisis swept through the company. The industry began to perceive Microsoft as a company that was in trouble, even though most of this trouble had been created by Microsoft itself.

Instead of imploding, though, Microsoft started to assume a "wartime" atmosphere. Led by Gates, the major executives and key engineers began to see their troubles as challenges, instead of threats. Much of this attitude was simply a reflection of Bill Gates's character and the corporate character that he had created.

One Microsoft engineer later said that at this time in the company's history, "You felt like you were at the center of the universe. It was an invigorating feeling. All this yanking by Bill was the price you paid to be there."

Finally, on May 22 of 1990, Bill Gates announced the "birthday" of Windows. In a closed-circuit television presentation in thirteen cities around the world, six thousand journalists were introduced to Windows.

The drama of this unveiling was unprecedented in the

industry. All of Gates's mistakes had been converted into advantages. Gates's insistence on perfection, his introduction of Windows as a solo product, and the repeated delays had all heightened the impact that Windows made.

Almost overnight, the price of Microsoft stock rocketed, and Bill Gates soon became the richest man in America, with a net worth recently estimated at $20 billion.

Bill Gates hadn't been afraid to stumble. And his nerve, and good sense, had made him wealthy beyond belief.

ASK YOURSELF

- What were the three biggest mistakes you made in the last five years? What did they teach you, and how have you changed your operations in response to them?
- What would you do if your most valued subordinate made a major mistake?
- What do you think your superior would do if you made a major mistake?

CHAPTER SIX

REWRITING THE RULES OF ENGAGEMENT

"A little rebellion, now and then, is a good thing."
—Thomas Jefferson

"I'm not a renegade. I'm a revolutionary."
—Ted Turner

While leading SEAL Team Six, my elite group of counterterrorists, I once contacted an overseas base commander during an operation designed to eliminate terrorists who were threatening his base.

I told him that our existing rules of engagement—which had been set by the local U.S. ambassador—were too restrictive. We needed more leeway to get down and dirty.

"The ambassador applied your restrictions for important political reasons," the commander fumed.

"Sir, we've *tried* it your way," I said, "and it hasn't

1 0 9

worked. If you want us to get these guys, you've got to untie our hands."

"No can do, Captain!"

"Which would you rather have, sir?" I barked. "A happy ambassador, or a pile of corpses in your compound?"

He pissed and moaned, then caved in. I didn't really care what he had to say, though; I was going to rewrite the rules, regardless. Hell, every tough competitor does that—not just counterterrorists.

In fact, it's imperative that you continually rewrite the rules of engagement throughout the operational phase of your project.

You've got to keep confounding your competitors, surprising them with innovations and variations. You've also got to keep challenging the written and unwritten rules that govern your industry, trying to bend the rules to your advantage. And you've got to keep changing the rules within your own organization, discarding restrictive regulations and guidelines, and updating all your tactics. It's the only way to be a winner—and to stay a winner.

As I said in the second chapter, you've got to begin a project by trying to dictate rules of engagement that work in your favor. But by the time you reach the operational phase of your project, you'll find that the initial rules you dictated—to your opponent and to your own team—no longer offer you as much of an advantage as you'd probably like.

For one thing, your opponent will have adjusted to these rules. He'll have whittled away at the rules that favor you, or will have done an end run around them.

Also, you'll find that as time has passed, *many* other factors will have changed. The environment of your battle will have been altered—often, by the very fact of your success. If the initial rules of engagement allowed you to become the top dog, you can bet that the government, or the press, or the labor unions, or your suppliers will want to bring you down a notch, to serve their own agendas.

You'll also find that success will create selfishness and complacency within your *own* company. Some of your people will want to satisfy their personal ambitions, and others will use success as an excuse to slack off.

When any of these things happen, it's time to rewrite the rules of engagement.

Whoever gets hurt by your rewrite of the rules will probably try to oppose you. They'll dig in their heels and tell you what a bully and a cheat you are. Well, fuck 'em. You didn't *invent* the concept of renegotiating a contract or revising a strategy. People have always changed the rules, and always will.

Whoever will suffer from your rewrite will try to make you think not only that it's *unfair* of you to change the existing rules but will also probably try to argue that the reigning rules somehow represent *morality*.

Don't fall for it. Most rules—even those that are

couched in terms of morality—are not moral absolutes. For example, throughout most of America's history, gambling was considered by the government to be immoral and was therefore generally illegal. But now most governments are heavily involved in the gambling industry, as sponsors of state lotteries, and so they've decided gambling isn't immoral after all.

Even if the existing rules *are* based on morality, remember that morality *changes* when conflicts *escalate*. Winston Churchill discovered this as a young soldier in India, fighting militant Moslems. Initially, he wouldn't allow his men to use the new "dumdum" bullet, remarking that "the bullet's shattering effects are simply appalling. I believe no such bullet has ever been used on human beings before, but only on game—stags, tigers, etc."

But as the conflict escalated, Churchill's troops began to encounter the full barbarity of the enemy, who began to attack field hospitals and to torture to death all of the wounded and sick soldiers as well as all their doctors and nurses.

Churchill then began to allow the use of dumdum bullets. "I feel rather a vulture," he said. "The only excuse is that I might myself become the carrion."

General Douglas MacArthur faced similar depravity in his enemy as he conquered the islands of the Pacific near the end of World War II. The Japanese forces under the control of the imperial government were notoriously bloodthirsty and paid no heed to the war's rules of engagement. Each of MacArthur's victories was unusually painful.

Having directly experienced the enemy's ferocity, MacArthur urged President Roosevelt to insist that after Hitler's defeat the Russians enter the war against Japan. At this time, the atomic bomb was not considered to be a viable solution to ending the war against Japan. The bomb had yet to be tested, and the overwhelming consensus among America's top military men was that the bomb would not work.

MacArthur was convinced that America needed Russia's help to defeat Japan.

When the European war ended, FDR did demand Russian help against Japan, at the Yalta Conference. In order to secure Russia's help, Roosevelt made several major concessions, which haunted the United States for years. Conventional wisdom has long held that Roosevelt made the concessions because he was weak and ill. In reality, though, he made the concessions in exchange for Stalin's secret pledge that sixty Russian divisions would be committed to the Japanese ground war.

However, before the invasion of Japan could begin, the atomic bomb was tested, and to the surprise of the U.S. military high command, it worked.

Thus, Roosevelt's successor, Harry Truman, faced an agonizing decision. He had to decide if America would violate the most basic rule of engagement in that war: the rule against purposeful mass killing of civilians. America had already killed thousands of civilians while bombing

Germany, but most of those deaths had inadvertently occurred during the bombing of military targets. The very essence of the atomic bomb, however, assured that no matter what its official military target, it would kill and maim countless civilians for miles around, and destroy entire cities.

Nonetheless, it was becoming increasingly clear to Truman, based upon Soviet actions in Europe, that Russia was beginning to be as great a threat to America as Japan was. Therefore, Truman no longer wanted Russia to help conquer Japan because Russia would then occupy at least half of Japan, as it had occupied half of Germany.

In addition, Truman wanted to *show* Russia—graphically and starkly—the new atomic power America held. And he wanted to convince them we weren't afraid to use it.

He dropped the bomb. And when he did, he forever rewrote the global rules of engagement.

Truman's decision to change the existing rules was painful because of the moral issues involved. In business, though, most of the rules you must rewrite will not involve difficult moral issues. For the most part, your war will simply be against the spirit-killing tyranny of the status quo.

Sometimes, you won't have enough power to *rewrite* existing rules, but that still doesn't mean you should follow them. In the 1950s and 1960s, Dr. Martin Luther King, Jr. and other civil rights advocates *broke* the existing rules that enforced segregation. They suffered terrible consequences. But by breaking these rules, Dr. King eventually forced their elimination.

Be steadfast in your fight against bullshit rules! Break them! Rewrite them! And move on.

> **ROGUETOID:** **When you rewrite the rules of engagement, your reasons better be damn good—because if the results are not, your reasons will be all you'll have left.**

Lessons from War

SEAL Team Six needed cars. And when an elite counter-terrorist force needs cars, we're not talking about Yugo hatchbacks. We're talking about cars that can withstand a mortar shot, jump over a building, and speak Hungarian.

My administrative commanding officer told me to requisition some off-the-rack military vehicles. But I suggested, as politely as possible, that he go fuck himself. No way was I going to send my men after terrorists in standard-issue Navy cars with Navy license plates. Why not just paint bull's-eyes on them? I needed civilian cars.

My administrative CO reminded me that the Navy had strict rules governing the procurement of vehicles and asked me if I was "too good to follow the rules." I assured him that I was.

Next day, I leapfrogged the chain of command and got

a three-star to authorize the purchase of a half dozen Jeep Eagles. I'd long before learned that if you want to bust past bullshit rules, you have to go straight to the top. In almost any organization, it's only the powerful people who can say "yes," and it's the pipsqueaks who can only say "no."

I took our Eagles on an overseas mission, but I was disappointed to discover that—contrary to what our intelligence had told us—in Europe and Asia, Eagles stuck out like sore dicks. There just weren't enough of them on the road, and they immediately identified us as Americans. I needed a more "international" car. Volkswagen? International—but slow and tinny. Audi? International—but ugly. Mercedes? Yes!

Of course, half a dozen Mercedes would *cost* far more than Navy rules allowed. So it was time to rewrite the rules again.

After some heavy-duty bitching and some creative requisitioning, I got my hands on three new Mercedes sedans and three Mercedes jeeps. Beautiful cars—but not beautiful enough for me. I needed to turn them into *fighting machines.*

I wanted each of them to have a blue police light that we could use in emergencies. It had to be hidden though, because we were customizing the cars in Germany, and German law strictly prohibited use of police lights by anyone but the proper authorities. However, if I wasn't going to blindly follow Navy rules, I sure as hell wasn't going to be bothered by German rules.

I also added firing ports for Heckler & Koch 9mm

machine guns on the sides of the cars. Then I put on a roof that held a modified tank turret. I also installed a special communications package that included a hidden satellite system. Finally, I bulked up the frames and suspensions so much that we could take the cars over Niagara Falls if we wanted. Not exactly "street legal," but so what?

Practically all this stuff violated *somebody's* rules and regulations, but I couldn't be deterred by that. When possible, I adjusted our military guidelines to allow for the changes I made, or I browbeat a superior officer into signing off on a rule variance. I also got some special clearances from the German Border Police Counterterrorist Team—GSG9.

As you can see, I didn't break the rules with a totally cavalier attitude; I just broke them.

But it all paid off the night the admiral came to visit.

We were working out of a naval base in Italy, on the Fourth of July, and we were assigned to bodyguard a visiting admiral. He was there to preside over an Independence Day celebration, and the Navy PR hacks had made a big deal out of his visit, which had resulted in about six death threats against him from the various terrorist groups that seem to coagulate around the Mediterranean. That's why we were brought in.

There were threats from the Red Brigade, Baader-Meinhof, some Basque terrorists, and a couple of Middle Eastern splinter groups. Some of them might have just been busting our balls to ruin our Fourth. But there were probably other groups who were also hoping to get a shot at the admiral but had been smart enough not to announce it. This was one of those years when it seemed like every terrorist in the world was pissed off at the United States and wanted nothing more than to disrupt our overseas activities.

The night of the Fourth, I was on edge. There was a big fireworks show just outside the base, in an unsecured area, and the conditions were ideal for a hit against the admiral. The fireworks were a perfect screen for an attack. You could have had a dozen bullets in your ass before you'd even realize they weren't errant cherry bombs.

As soon as I could, I pulled the admiral away from the festivities and hustled him into one of our Mercedes. He was a tough old bastard, a real straight shooter, and he understood the need for caution.

We headed back to the base in a convoy—all six Mercedes—with the admiral in the fifth car, and me and a SEAL named Baby Rich taking the point.

Two klicks down the road I spotted it: a roadblock, made out of two Volkswagen vans parked end to end. Off to both sides of the roadblock, barely visible, were rifle barrels. Behind our convoy, a big-ass black pickup came barreling down the road. I had to assume it was theirs. No turning back.

I couldn't figure out how they'd known we had the admiral with us. These guys were good.

Within seconds, I had all six Mercedes on a guarded-channel, secure radio band, and I ordered the men to bring out their heavy ordnance.

"Car two, pull alongside us!" I yelled as Baby Rich positioned himself at the roof with a 9mm machine gun.

When the second car was door-to-door with us, Baby Rich and the shooter in car two opened up. Two lines of fire flew toward the blockade, straight as lasers.

"Ramming speed!" I screamed. I peeled out, and so did the Mercedes next to me. Bullets started to chip and chink our thick Plexiglas windshields.

"Car three and car four, flank left-right," I yelled, and the third and fourth cars veered to the far shoulders of the road, where each of them could get clear shots with their side-port H&K's.

Next thing I knew, car two and my car simultaneously slammed into the Volkswagens, and they split apart like a dam bursting. As we crashed through, we laid a wall of fire on the stunned bastards in the ditches beside the road.

"That's why I will *not* drive a Vee-dub!" I crowed. "No *heft* to 'em."

The rest of the convoy blasted through what was left of the blockade before the terrorists even had time to die.

We all flipped up our blue police lights and didn't slow down until we got inside the gates of the base.

I opened the door for the admiral, and by then, he was grinning. "Damn, that was a helluva ride!" he said. He shook my hand and gazed fondly at our fleet of Mercedes. "Son," he said, "where in the *hell* did you get all this . . . stuff?"

"Sears Roebuck Auto Center, sir!" I smiled.

"Well, give my regards to Mr. Sears and Mr. Roebuck."

1 1 9

"Yes, sir!"

After that, I had another friend in a high place. And when you rewrite rules as often as I did, that helps.

Lessons from Business, and from the Lives of Successful People

In 1973, the best runner in America—probably the best runner in American history—was flat-ass broke. Steve Prefontaine, a young man of incredible character, owned seven official American records and several other, more esoteric records—fastest three-mile with a 103-degree fever, fastest 5,000 with a foot lacerated to the bone, and fastest mile in agricultural field-burning smoke so dense and dark it caused a hundred-car pileup. One magazine had called Prefontaine "the most popular athlete in the world." But in an era of millionaire jocks, the great athlete lived in a shitty little trailer near a putrid-smelling lumber mill.

Of course, Prefontaine was in a sport that had no professional league, but that wasn't the root cause of his poverty. In other countries, runners lived regally off government stipends or corporate sponsorship. In America, however, this was against the rules. The governing body of American track and field, the Amateur Athletic Union, decreed that no track athlete was allowed to profit from the sport in any way.

Prefontaine, though, was the national leader of a revolt

against the AAU's archaic rules. He railed against the AAU in the media, with the full support of his coach, Bill Bowerman, a former major with the Army's Tenth Mountain Division. Bowerman had fought in World War II on skis in the Alps.

While Prefontaine openly fought the AAU's rules, he and Bowerman also did an end run around them. Bowerman helped Prefontaine get a job in a local sports shoe store that was part of a small start-up company Bowerman co-owned. The store sold running shoes that featured a special sole Bowerman had invented.

Prefontaine didn't exactly *do* much at the store but was paid a salary anyway. Thus, he was able to move out of his trailer.

Bowerman, a staunchly moral man of high character, had no compunction about tweaking the AAU rules, even though the AAU styled itself as the sport's bastion of morality.

As an "unpaid favor" to Bowerman's small company, Prefontaine agreed to wear Bowerman's shoes in his races. This was, strictly speaking, *not* an endorsement, which would have been against AAU rules. Bowerman customized a pair of shoes for Prefontaine, and Prefontaine brought them to a race. At the last minute, Bowerman taped the company logo onto the shoes.

Prefontaine was so fast, though, that the logo—a streamlined "swoosh" symbol—flew off the shoes, which Bowerman and his partner, Phil Knight, called Nikes.

Prefontaine's support of the fledgling Nike Company was critically important to the company's early survival. Nike soon abandoned the shoe store and made all its money selling shoes wholesale to other stores. The company became tremendously successful.

About ten years later, though, Nike was in jeopardy. By November of 1984, its stock had sunk from a high of $28.00 per share to $6.60. That same month marked the first quarter in which Nike recorded a loss (of $2.5 million). It was the fifth consecutive quarter of declining revenues. The company laid off four hundred people, including one-third of the promotions department. It cut its endorsement contracts with athletes by almost half. And 1985 looked like it would be even worse.

Phil Knight, who was by this time running Nike without Bowerman's help, told his top associate, Rob Strasser, that he wanted to risk the company's future on one enormous endorsement contract. Of course, this broke Nike's own rule of cutting back during hard times, but Knight was an inveterate rule breaker.

The athlete that Knight and Strasser chose to gamble on was a young man who had begun playing pro basketball about a month earlier. *Forbes* magazine ran an article ridiculing the shaky Nike corporation for lavishing a $2.5 million endorsement deal on a rookie named Michael Jordan.

The next task Nike faced was designing shoes for Jordan. Standard industry practice dictated that the shoe design should be strong, masculine, and understated: *jock* shoes. But Knight broke the design rules by approving garish red-and-black shoes that looked like they belonged in a cartoon.

When the directors of the National Basketball Association saw the shoes, they hit the roof. The NBA was, at that time, struggling to overcome the widely held perception that its overpaid, often uncontrollable athletes were little more than drug-addled exhibitionists—and these wild shoes *sent the wrong message.* The NBA ruled that Jordan could not wear the shoes in league games.

Jordan called Rob Strasser and told him the bad news. Strasser asked Jordan what the NBA would do if Jordan broke the rule banning the shoes.

Jordan told Strasser that he'd be fined $1,000 per game.

"Wear 'em," said Strasser. "We'll cover you."

Jordan wore the shoes, and the NBA levied the fine.

The fine brought immediate attention to the shoes. A Chicago sportswriter wrote, "Michael Jordan is not the most incredible, the most colorful, the most amazing, the most flashy, or the most mind-boggling thing in the NBA. His shoes are."

Strasser was delighted with the controversy. It strongly projected the rebellious, break-the-rules image that Nike loved.

The conventional approach would have been to stick with the shoes, absorb the fine, and milk the publicity. But Strasser and Knight again played contrarian.

They told Jordan to stop wearing the shoes in games. Then they released a TV ad of Jordan wearing his red-and-black shoes while a voice-over intoned: "On September fifteenth, Nike created a revolutionary new basketball shoe. On October eighteenth, the NBA threw them out of the game. Fortunately, the NBA can't keep you from wearing them. Air Jordans from Nike."

Shortly after the commercial hit the air, Strasser brought a four-man team of Nike executives into his office and gave them the job of expanding the Michael Jordan line of merchandise. He told them, "On this rock, we will build a church."

Nike recovered. And Nike *prospered*: by rewriting its own rules and defying everyone else's.

As I've shown in the last two chapters, day-to-day success—in the *operational phase* of your project— demands strict adherence to the same values that you honored in the planning and training stages of your project: boldness, willingness to write your own rules, courage, character, and creativity. These values not only *create* successful projects but also nurture projects once they're up and running.

I believe that, just as rules are made to be broken, values are made to be followed.

Now it's time to march forward once more.

In the next section, I'm going to tell you how to *maintain* success.

Ready! March! Attack the system!

ASK YOURSELF

- What, other than fear, is stopping you from rewriting your own company's rules of engagement?
- Do you feel more constricted by your *industry's* rules of engagement, or by your *own company's* rules of engagement?
- What company most recently rewrote the rules of engagement in your industry? How did they benefit?

PART 4

MAINTAINING SUCCESS— THE ROGUE WARRIOR WAY

CHAPTER SEVEN

YOU CAN'T KEEP IT IF YOU DON'T RISK IT

"It's the risk that makes the chase exciting."
—General George Patton

"Once the dice have left your hands, there's nothing to do but watch how they come up."
—General Colin Powell

"I rode my grey pony all along the skirmish line when everyone else was lying down in cover. Foolish, perhaps, but I play for high stakes."
—Winston Churchill

There's no way to just *hang on* to success. Every day you *gain* some new success, and every day you *lose* some of your old success. You can no more *retain* success than you can breathe by sucking in a deep breath and holding it.

Therefore, your goal must be to *gain* more success each day than you lose. And how do you do that?

You do it the same way you gained your first success at the beginning of your career: *by taking risks.*

Show me a man who takes no risks and I'll show you a man whose enterprises—whatever they may be—are stagnant. And if your enterprises are stagnant, sooner or later you'll lose them. If you're wealthy, maybe it will take a long time for your resources to dwindle. Maybe you'll even be lucky enough to die before your assets run out. But at some point, if you're not *taking chances* and making *new* money, you or your heirs will be flat-ass broke. Inflation *alone* will see to that. And whatever inflation doesn't take, your competitors will.

Unfortunately, though, the American business community now seems to be scared to death of risk. The way I see it, American business has become more afraid to take risks than other industrial powers, chiefly Japan and Germany, because we've become too fat and satisfied, and because our focus on short-term profits has made us shy away from anything that won't pay off immediately.

Also, our major companies are now so bureaucratized that most executives are afraid to *fart* without first circulating a memo asking permission.

This fear of risk has undercut innovation in America and is part of the reason why Japan has surpassed us at discovering new, ingenious methods of production. If we weren't so goddamned afraid to take a few chances, Japan would never have dominated manufacture of the

1 3 0

American inventions of the transistor or the VCR, just by risking money on R&D until they found better ways to build them.

Furthermore, being "risk averse," as the economists say—or "chickenshit," as I put it—does more than just kill innovation in industrial processes. It also kills part of the human spirit. Hell, it's *fun* to take risks. If it wasn't, gambling wouldn't have been a popular form of recreation throughout human history. Taking risks excites the spirit and rekindles our hope for a better life.

General Patton once said, "The whole joy of life is taking chances, to build enough faith to destroy all our fears. That is why gambling is so much fun. And the highest form of gambling is combat with an enemy that wants to kill you. You can never gamble any higher stakes!"

Like anything else that is exciting and invigorating, risk can bring out the best in a man. Obviously, it can inspire and nourish his courage. Less obviously, but just as certainly, risk also gives rise to creativity and decisiveness.

James Burke, the CEO of Johnson & Johnson, has noted that, "What we needed more than anything else at J&J was a climate that would encourage people to take risks." Burke recalled that when he first began working at J&J, he developed a risky product that failed miserably. He was called into the office of General Johnson, the founder of the company. Burke was afraid he'd be fired because he'd cost the company millions of dollars. But

1 3 1

when Burke entered the office, Johnson stood to shake his hand and said, "I want to congratulate you. The hardest job I have is getting people to make *decisions*. If you make that *same* wrong decision again, I'll fire you. But I hope you'll make a lot of others, and that you'll understand there are going to be more failures than successes."

Thomas Watson Jr., the head of IBM, once dealt similarly with an exec who'd pissed away $10 million on a risky endeavor. The guy offered to resign. "Not on your life," said Watson. "You think I'll let you go now, after spending ten million dollars on your education?"

Burke and Watson, however, accepted these failures only because their subordinates had taken *reasonable* risks. If you don't take calculated, smart risks, you're just a fool who'll soon self-destruct. Remember, before you take *any* gamble, you've got to have a clear vision, a goal, a thoughtful plan, and a stacked deck. If the odds are strongly against you, hold back. If you play against bad odds, you're not a risk taker, you're a degenerate gambler, and the law of averages will quickly grind you to dust.

Even if the odds do favor you, be damn careful about *how much* you risk. Don't risk what you can't afford to lose. Risk only your *marginal* assets, because if you lose them, you'll still be in the game. Don't "bet the farm," even on a sure thing—because there's no such *thing* as a sure thing. The more something *looks* like a sure thing, the more likely it is to be a trap or a scam.

Also, never bet your money when you can, instead, bet your time. Try to be the *ramrod* of a project, not the *banker*. Invest *your* time and *their* money. You can always find more time—it's called *working longer hours*. But you *can't* always find more money. When it's gone, it's gone.

The time you give, though, has got to represent the *best* of you. It's got to fully reflect your vision, your training, your planning, and your character. You've got to give your heart and soul to a project to be equal to your investors.

When you can, *spread* your risks. It always shocks me when some dumb-ass consolidates his stock market holdings into just one stock, on the premise that he *knows so much* about that stock. Don't forget that every time you buy a share of stock—because you're *sure* it will go up—the person selling the share is just as sure it will go down. And he probably knows just as much as you do.

And don't forget this: *Not* taking risks is every bit as risky as taking them. Consider General McClellan, Lincoln's chickenshit leader of the Union Army, who sat on his ass with 150,000 soldiers while Robert E. Lee trembled on the other side of the Potomac with a far smaller force. Lee was certain McClellan would come kick his ass and end the war in a month. But it gradually became obvious that McClellan had no intention of fighting until the odds were *overwhelmingly* in his favor. Lincoln, who accused McClellan of being afflicted with "the slows," finally gave up on his general and hired someone else.

But by then, Lee was ready. Lee had gained time to amass more men and more artillery. In fact, Lee had gotten his extra artillery by melting down twelve-pound howitzers and recasting them as six-pounders. Of course, during this process, Lee had rendered himself virtually devoid of artillery. But when Lee melted his guns, it was winter—a poor time for McClellan to attack—and Lee had also come to realize that McClellan was a coward.

The risk paid off. The war went on, and the badly outmatched South came close to winning.

Don't be a McClellan. Be a Lee. Be bold. Take risks. *Perpetuate* your success.

> **ROGUETOID:** **There is only one kind of failure I cannot tolerate: the failure to risk failure.**

Lessons from War

Officially, the mission of my team was to "aid the stabilization of democracy" in an equatorial African country. Unofficially, our mission was to shoot and loot our way into a terrorist compound and free a hostage. The hostage was the newly elected vice-chairman of the African country's parliament. I can't tell you the name of the country because this was a "black-op" that's sched-uled to be held in classified files until the year 2015. Suffice it to say, it was a hot, shitty, poverty-inflamed country—which could be just about any country in that part of the world.

The vice-chairman was being held by a tribal separa-tist group that had splintered off from a significantly larger body of rebels. Our intelligence reports said there were only about twelve men in the clique. That was good. Their small size decreased our risk—and this project was *full* of risk.

The separatists said they were willing to return the vice-chairman for a ransom of $1 million, which was big money to them. But the president of the country—who hated the parliament anyhow—decreed that he wouldn't negotiate with terrorists. To me, it seemed like a hoity-toity attitude for a country that changed leaders about as often as I changed socks, but it sounded good to our State Department, so off we went, into darkest Africa.

I devised the extraction operation myself, with input from my men. On my team, everybody got to put in their two cents because everybody's ass was on the line. But ultimately, the major decisions were mine. That was *my* idea of a stable democracy.

I could come up with only one viable strategy for making physical contact with the vice-chairman, who was being held deep in the jungle. Somebody would have to offer his own butt as bait and walk right into the "lion's den." I nominated myself, seconded the nomina-

tion, and then elected me. On my teams, I never appointed somebody else to do the dirtiest jobs. I led from
the front.

The plan called for me to notify the separatists,
through a communications channel they'd already
opened, that I was coming into their territory with the
ransom money. We'd tell them that I would have
$500,000 on me, and that they'd get the rest when they
escorted me and the vice-chairman to the outskirts of the
country's capital. In reality, I would have only a small
sum on me. But I'd also be carrying a satellite tracking
device, which would let my men know where I was.
Then my guys would parachute in and bust out me and
the vice-chairman.

It was a simple plan, which is my favorite kind, but
there were a lot of variables we might encounter, and
some would be dicey as hell. However, as I've said, war is
nothing but taking one calculated risk after another, and
this job was a *whole* lot like war.

Forty-eight hours after I finalized the plan, I was
chugging up a mud brown river in a rented civilian
motorboat. At a site I'd arranged with the separatists, I
pulled over and waited. I activated my locator. An hour
later, two skinny black men with Vietnam-era Soviet
rifles emerged silently from the undergrowth. I slowly
raised my hands.

One of them said, "De money."

I picked up a small leather bag and tossed it to him.
When he saw how little money was in it, he grimaced

and ordered me out of the boat. As I got out, his anger seemed to build, and he hit me in the gut with his rifle. Small price to pay for stabilizing democracy.

They patted me down and tossed my weapons and my tracking device into the river. Didn't matter. My guys would have a fix on my coordinates by now and would be in the air in an hour. My job now was to leave a trail they could follow. I was wearing boots with a special cat's paw design on the heel. That's what my squad would be looking for. There was a chance that Cheech and Chong here would erase our tracks as we went, but I doubted they were that smart.

We marched about a mile to a camp. I left my cat's paw tracks the whole way. A fucking Cub Scout could have followed our trail. In camp, they threw me in a hooch.

Outside, I could hear men arguing in a staccato jumble of syllables. They might have been deciding to kill me, but I doubted it. My presumption had been that when I stiffed them, they'd try to ransom me, too. My take on these punks was that money was their main concern.

Of course, I could've been wrong.

As I sat there, I tried to count the number of different voices, to get an idea of how many men were in the camp. I got the feeling that, as our intelligence had indicated, there weren't very many—which was *good*. I sure as hell didn't want my little squad walking into a *mob* of killers.

By my reckoning, my men should have been close by now. The plan had been for them to execute a high-altitude, low-opening parachute jump. A HALO jump is the best way to clandestinely penetrate a hostile area. The plane they would deploy from would be so high no one would hear it, and the men would free-fall as long as possible, so no one could see their chutes. Obviously, parachuting into a jungle was risky as hell, but my men were among the best in the world at difficult jumps. As I sat waiting, I thanked God that we had trained so hard for missions like this.

Before nightfall, the separatists brought the vice-chairman to my hooch, handcuffed and hobbled. Together, we were easier to guard. Right off the bat, he started bitching about my not bringing enough money.

"You're welcome," I said.

My men were due at 2100 hours. But they didn't show. Shit! A SNAFU! I waited. Sweat rolled down my neck in fat drops.

Finally, after midnight, the racket started. I knocked the vice-chairman to the floor and laid on him until one of my men burst into the hooch. "Knock-knock," he said. "Are you decent?" I was glad as hell to see him.

"You're late," I said.

"Traffic was a bitch," he replied.

Before my guy could even toss me a gun, the noise outside was already dying down.

We hauled ass back to the river, where a helicopter was waiting for us. As we jumped onto the chopper, I felt that crazy, high rush of elation that comes with the overproduction of adrenaline and the escape from a bad situation.

Our risks had paid off. Once more, we had established ourselves as the best goddamn counterterrorist team in the world. And once more, we had shown the world that Uncle Sam, when necessary, could be one mean son of a bitch.

We were alive. We had succeeded. Life was good.

Lessons from Business, and from the Lives of Successful People

After Bob Dole got shot to hell in World War II, much of his body was practically dead. His right arm hung from his shoulder by a tangle of sinew, and his left arm wouldn't move. He couldn't control his bladder or bowels, and his legs were just weak pieces of warm meat.

But Dole was a man of incredible character, and he gradually gained the ability to lift his "good" arm a few inches off his chest. He forced his legs to learn to hobble, and he willed himself to regain control over his bodily functions.

But the damage to him was so profound that infection raged in practically every part of his body. His fevers got as high as 108 degrees. For months that stretched into years, he lay in Army hospitals, wasting into a skeleton.

Just before Christmas of 1945, Dole woke up with a searing pain in his chest. Because he was an invalid, he

1 3 9

had developed a blood clot in his lung. He was given a powerful anticoagulant that temporarily made him a hemophiliac. Also, the drug further weakened his immunity, and his fevers began to spike uncontrollably. Water collected in his lungs, and his breath rattled like that of a dying person. No drug could control the infection, so doctors packed Dole in ice to keep his brain from cooking.

One doctor mentioned an experimental drug Dole could try. The Army had the only supply of it, and it had been tried on just two patients. One had died, and the other had gone blind. Even if it worked, it was believed that it might leave Dole mentally retarded, paralyzed, deaf, or blind.

Dole took the risk. In the war, he'd learned to accept risk as a fact of life.

They gave him the new, experimental drug—streptomycin—and he went into a comalike condition for three days.

On the fourth day, he sat up in bed, and asked for a milk shake.

Dole never stopped taking risks and never stopped pushing himself far beyond his presumable limits. In doing so, he established himself as one of the great political leaders of the postwar era.

Another hero of World War II, the youngest flier in the entire Navy, was a skinny boy named George Bush. Late in the war, Bush was leading a bombing raid over the Japanese-controlled island of Chichi Jima when his plane was hit by heavy flak. Bush's plane began to pitch and heave, but he decided he could *probably* make it to his target before the plane went down. He calculated correctly, dropped his bombs, and headed off. Then Bush, twenty years old, had to decide whether to land the plane and face capture, or ditch it in the sea and take his chances there. He decided that the shark-filled ocean was a safer bet.

He flew as far as his plane would go and then ejected, slamming into his aircraft's tail as he bailed out. His head was ripped open, and his chute was sliced, but he made it down and was later picked up by a submarine.

When Bush returned to his patrician family after the war, he had many offers of soft jobs in the various family businesses, but he turned them all down. The war had toughened him, and he was ready to take a shot at making it on his own. After all, what was the risk? Bankruptcy? Big deal.

So he traveled to a godforsaken part of the Texas plain where drilling for oil was virtually the only existing business.

Bush became an "independent oilman," which was basically a synonym for "gambler." He didn't have the sponsorship of one of the major oil companies, nor did he work in one of the safe, oil-allied industries, such as equipment servicing, which made millions of dollars off the gamblers.

For a couple of years, Bush learned the business and

had his ups and downs. Then he approached the most successful oil wildcatter in the area and proposed a partnership. The other oilman took the offer—on the condition that Bush would bring half a million dollars to the business.

Bush went home and raised the money from his wealthy family.

Then Bush and his new partner took an extravagant risk. They bet their entire wad—$850,000, between the two of them—on one eight-thousand-acre oil lease.

Before they did it, though, Bush studied the *hell* out of the land they were leasing. He learned every conceivable thing he could about the deal. It wasn't a sure bet, but the odds of at least breaking even were excellent, and the downside appeared to be somewhat limited.

But if every possible element of the risk turned to shit, they would lose their money, and Bush probably wouldn't be able to go home for more. After all, Bush's family was supportive—but not stupid.

They drilled seventy-one holes. All seventy-one hit. They began to make about a million and a half dollars a year.

Barely thirty, George Bush was a wealthy man, in his own right.

He began a career in politics.

About thirty-five years later, President George Bush faced the greatest risk of his political life: facing down Saddam Hussein in Iraq.

But when Bush first drew his "line in the sand" and defied Hussein to cross it, he was taking an enormous risk. In the early days of the confrontation, Bush did not have enough troops in the area to stop an attack by Hussein. One analyst said, quite accurately, that the U.S. troops would be little more than "speed bumps" if Hussein chose to roll his Iraqi tank divisions across the Kuwaiti-Saudi border.

But Hussein hesitated. And hesitated—as Bush rushed in reinforcements.

Hussein was, in effect, playing McClellan to Bush's Lee.

Then Bush and his generals enacted the famous end run around the immobile Iraqi forces. It was a bold, innovative, and risky maneuver. It was also brilliantly effective.

George Bush had learned, at an early age, that you can't maintain success by just hanging on to what you have. You've got to risk, risk, and risk again.

All great leaders are great risk takers.

And that leads us to our next chapter. It's on leadership.

In business and in life, you can't lead by *taking votes* and following popular demand. When you lead, you lead *alone*.

Even if a business is successful, it won't survive for long without a strong, independent leader.

Ready to attack a new chapter? Good!

Attack!

ASK YOURSELF

- What would you have to risk to take your company to the next level? What's the risk of not doing this?
- Who is the biggest risk taker in your company? Has his ascent been faster than yours?
- What was your greatest achievement that did not involve risk?

CHAPTER EIGHT

LEAD FROM THE FRONT

"Some single mind must be master, else there will be no agreement in anything."

—Abraham Lincoln

"When in charge, be in charge."
—General Max Thurman

"If you're not alone at the head of your troops, you're not leading."

—Me

Once upon a time, most leaders were *rulers*. They were kings. They had absolute power. They had glamour.

Those days are gone. The kings are mostly dead. Now, most leaders are just . . . the guys in front. And now, there's only one way for most of us to be a leader—by stepping forward, taking a stand, and inspiring others to follow.

In America today, being a leader means fighting in the forward positions. It means standing alone at the head of

1 4 5

your troops. It means putting your cause and your people first, and yourself second.

In short, being a leader isn't very glamorous anymore, and it usually doesn't mean having absolute power. But that's good. All that glamour and all that dictatorial power was *bullshit*. It didn't *work*. If it *did,* we'd still *have* a lot of kings around.

Sometimes, you still see certain CEOs, and certain politicians, trying to act like kings. But most of them don't last long. The only absolute rulers with any job security these days are Third World dictators, like Saddam Hussein—and those guys tend to end up dead.

At some organizations these days, though, there's a *different* source of tyranny. It's *rule by committee,* and it's just as hobbling as a monarchy. Some so-called leaders *like* rule-by-committee because it relieves them of responsibility and makes them feel like they're real *democratic.* The trouble with democracies, though, is that too often nothing gets *done* in them, or they end up being like three wolves and a sheep voting on what to have for lunch.

If you want your project to *continue* to operate effectively, day after day, year after year, you've got to steer clear of both kingships and committees. You've got to run your company the hard way—by doing the dirty, dangerous jobs *yourself* and setting an example that others will *want* to follow. You've got to be a "servant leader."

George Patton once said, "Trying to lead men from

behind makes you a driver, not a leader. It is easier to *lead* men, just as it is easier to *drag* a log chain. You cannot *push* a log chain, and you cannot *push* troops. The troops will keep running back to you for instructions, and because of fear. A leader must be up *front*. You've got to know what's going on."

Once, in World War II, Patton's troops were preparing to cross a river. Patton entered his headquarters and found his engineers studying maps of the river. "Cross here," Patton said, pointing at a spot on the map. The engineers distractedly informed Patton that they couldn't do that because they didn't know how deep the river was there.

"Hell," said Patton, pointing to the waterline on his pants, "it's *this* deep."

As Patton demonstrated, wading into problems *ahead* of your troops is the best way to know *exactly* what you're getting them into. You won't have to rely on abstract reports and misleading statistics.

Also, if your people see you actually doing the same work they do, and straining the same muscles they strain, it will change your workplace forever. Your people will respect you more, and—when you discover how hard their jobs are—you'll respect *them* more.

And if you look like you're *enjoying* their work, you'll help them to *appreciate* their jobs more. Wal-Mart founder Sam Walton, who was the richest man in America when he died, used to go for delivery rides with Wal-Mart truckers, just because he found it "so much fun." How do you think that made his fleet of drivers feel?

Probably more important, and better understood—and I imagine it also made them feel like they had pretty damn good jobs.

In addition, leading your troops from the front is the best possible test of your *own commitment* to your cause. If your cause doesn't merit *your* pain, it's probably not worth fighting for.

Furthermore, if you're suffering alongside your troops, you'll be much more likely to make the tough decisions of leadership as *quickly* and *forcefully* as possible.

It's often painful to lead from the front, by yourself. To be a leader who shoulders responsibility and decision making alone means having people constantly second-guess you and tell you what a dumb shit you are. It means risking your job and—in the military—your life. It means having superiors who need scapegoats, and it frequently means looking in vain for people to help.

That's why *character* is so important. Without character, a leader won't last a single day in the forward positions.

Abraham Lincoln often suffered alongside his troops. He frequently visited the war front, and once he was shot at, becoming the only sitting president ever to see action. Another time, he was forced to don a disguise to escape danger.

This proximity to the pain of war spurred Lincoln to waste no time in reaching the many monumental decisions that marked his presidency. Lincoln, in fact, was so boldly decisive that he rewrote the rules that governed the presidency. He *vastly* expanded presidential power by starting the first American draft, by declaring martial law, by personally directing the war effort, and by spending federal money without the approval of Congress. After Lincoln, the presidency was a far more potent office.

Lincoln was savaged by the press and by other politicians for this bold exercise of power. But he steadfastly clung to his authority. He argued to one group of congressmen, "Gentlemen, suppose all your gold was placed into the hands of one man, to cross the Niagara River on a rope. Would you shake the cable and shout, 'Stoop a little more, go faster, go slower, lean a little!' No. You would hold your breath, as well as your tongue, and keep your hands off until he got safely over."

Lincoln, however, was able to achieve his unprecedented level of power, in part, because he was extraordinarily open to suggestion. He was a great listener. He was truly empathetic. He was notably humble and never exercised power for pleasure, or for self-aggrandizement.

Within his own cabinet, Lincoln encouraged diverse opinion, and for years accepted the acerbic presence of the ballbusting Treasury Secretary Salmon P. Chase (whom some conspiracy buffs think was eventually involved in Lincoln's murder).

In urging debate, Lincoln predated one of modern America's most successful business leaders, Michael Eisner, who made the once-weak Disney empire the most powerful entertainment conglomerate in the world.

Eisner is known to demand, when no one opposes his point of view, "Why is there no *conflict* at this meeting? Something's *wrong* when there's no conflict."

Remember this, though: If taking somebody else's advice leads you to a world of shit, don't blame *them*. It was *their* advice, but it was *your* decision.

On the other hand, if somebody else's advice results in a victory, give them all the credit.

That may not be *fair* to *you*, but what do you want, fairness or success?

Anyhow, if you're *really* a good leader, after you've won your battle, every shooter you've got will naturally *assume* that *he* was the key to victory. And, by God, he won't be too far wrong.

As Lao Tzu said long ago, "Fail to honor people, and they will fail to honor you. But of a good leader, who talks little, when his work is done, his aim fulfilled, they will say, '*We did this ourselves.*'"

ROGUETOID: It's not lonely at the *top*. It's lonely at the *front*.

Lessons from War

I was sitting alone at the bar of a South American cantina, tossing down Cuervos and chewing limes, peel and all, when a priest came in and sat next to me. Not my usual type of drinking buddy.

"May I talk to you a moment?" he asked. He had a warm smile but big sad eyes. I lifted my shot glass to him, nodded yes, and threw down another Cuervo. "We need—our mission needs—your help," he said.

I pushed a twenty down the bar to him.

"We need *much* more than that," he insisted.

I grinned and slid him another twenty. "You got some big *huevos* on you, Father," I said.

But he didn't need money. He needed some people killed.

Actually, he'd have *much* preferred to have his enemies reformed, or arrested, or even removed to some other part of the world. But that wasn't going to happen. The people he feared were among the last remnants of the corrupt regime that had terrorized his country for the past fifteen years. They weren't going to change, they weren't going to leave, and a general amnesty protected them from arrest.

The priest's country had just held free elections, with the help of an American task force, which had included select members of SEAL Team Six. The country had kicked out the scum at the top. However, in various pockets around the country, small cadres of paramilitary thugs—who'd served the former regime as death squads—were still brutalizing the people who'd helped end their reign of terror. These assholes particularly hated the Catholic priests and nuns, who'd been instrumental in the revolt.

The priest told me about a nun at his mission who had been kidnapped the previous week by the local death squad and then returned—disfigured. The leader of the death squad had personally done most of the "work" on her, the priest said.

"We should not have to endure more from these people," he said simply. His eyes drilled into mine. He was a man of powerful presence, a strong moral leader.

He'd already gone to the authorities, he said, but they were afraid to get involved.

"The people in my village speak well of you," he said. I was surprised anybody here spoke of me at all. So far, all we'd done was guard some polling places and kick the ass of a mayor who was trying to throw the election.

"I'll talk to my men," I said. But I already knew what I was going to do, and I didn't need anybody's permission to do it.

Even so, I sure as hell needed some backup.

I convened a meeting of my men three hours later in the same cantina. The Dos Equis was on me because I had a big favor to ask. I wanted these men to risk their lives on a job that was beyond the official scope of our mission here.

When I started telling them about the priest, my men seemed to know where I was heading, and a couple of them wouldn't look me in the eye. So I laid it on thick— all the gory details about the nun, embroidering here and there, for effect. You might not think you'd have to *exaggerate* the horror of an incident like that, but these guys had seen everything.

After a while, I had them all on board. I'm a good salesman. These days, a strong leader *has* to be. You can *force* men to go on a mission, but if you do, you'll lose their hearts and souls, and sooner or later it will cost you your mission and maybe your life.

"One question, Captain," said Mickey Kalosh. "How the hell we gonna *find* these guys, without gettin' killed while we snoop around?"

"That's my job," I said.

"How come you get all the fun jobs?" Mickey asked.

"Cuz I'm the boss."

The next day, I drove into the small town where the priest believed the death squad was centered, and went straight to the dilapidated red-light district. Posing as an American businessman, I wore a polo shirt, nice slacks, and expensive loafers. I carried an eelskin briefcase. I began sampling the local libations and chatting up various lowlife characters. I let it be known that I was looking for muscle, to help me overcome a business competitor "the quick way."

Before the night was over, I'd made contact with a guy who appeared to be my target. He sure as hell *talked* like my target; every time I mentioned the new president, he spit on the floor. He told me that disposing of a business competitor would be "not a problem" and asked only $5,000 for the job.

I told him I'd meet him the next night with the money and with the itinerary of my competitor. I left the tavern first, then hid in my car across the street. When he came out, I followed him in my car and discovered that he lived on a ranch outside town. At the ranch house were half a dozen late-model cars. His cronies', I assumed.

That same night, I got with my priest and gave him a description of the man. I had the right guy.

I spent the next day talking to my men. I needed all their ideas because this looked to be an ugly hit. Like a lot of counterterrorist operations, it was more like police work than a military mission. We couldn't just call in the artillery. This had to be a surgical strike—limited in scope, swift, and unexpected.

We considered an ambush, and the possibility of trapping them in the house and waiting them out. But logistical and political concerns soon reduced our options. The only way to do it was to hit the house as a group, and overwhelm their resistance. Workable—but risky.

As our options dwindled, some of the guys seemed to lose their taste for it. One shooter, in particular, was feeling hinky. He was a young guy, new to the squad, and he hadn't yet seen how *good* we were at this kind of shit.

I stroked him and played cheerleader. But I was losing him. Finally, he said, "Captain, I think we should run this up the chain of command and see what they say."

I stood up and towered over him. "In SEAL Team Six, *I'm* the chain of command. And this operation is *go*. You in or out?"

"In," he said softly. If he'd said "out," I would've left him out of it. I was going to make this mission succeed, but I wasn't going to force anyone to help. I was a leader, not a dictator, and the most powerful force I had was the free will and the initiative of my men.

Eight hours later, at oh-dark-hundred, we squatted behind a car outside the ranch house. We saw their silhouettes through the windows and heard loud talk and laughter.

"If they surrender, take prisoners," I said. "If they resist, do your thing. We hit the door single file, then go left-right-left-right, as we enter."

"Who's first man through the door?" asked the new kid, nervously. He was probably afraid it was him; lots of units give the shit jobs to the fresh meat.

"Captain is," said Mickey Kalosh. "He *always* is."

The new kid gave me a special look. I've seen it enough to recognize it. It was respect. He seemed to calm down. "Watch my back," I said to him. He nodded and fell in right behind me.

We kicked the door and ran in screaming like banshees, to confuse and intimidate them. But these guys didn't scare. The house was a fucking arsenal, and every one of them was armed. They were good—but we were *better*. Maybe because we didn't do our training on nuns.

In seconds the house was quiet. It was also a bloody mess. Their blood, not ours. No loss to the world.

1 5 5

Then, from behind, I heard someone yell, "Down!" and I felt a foot in the small of my back pushing me toward the floor. As I went down, I heard a loud, windy hiss at the top of my head and I caught sight of a two-foot machete whizzing past. Then there was one more burble of automatic weapons fire, and a guy from an overhead loft dropped to the floor, with the machete still in his hands.

I looked behind me and saw the new kid. "Thanks," I said. But his eyes were still rattling around too fast for him to make conversation.

On the way back, we shared a gallon jug of Cuervo and felt the heat of the booze and the even warmer feeling you get when you and your men face down danger together and help each other overcome it.

Now we all had this mission in common, and we always would. It had started as *my* mission, but now it belonged to all of us, and that made me even prouder of it.

"We're a good team, aren't we?" said the new kid.

"Damn right," I said. "And when we get back to the cantina, the Dos Equis is on me."

"Fuck that," said the new kid. "That's how this whole thing got *started*."

"Okay, then, it's on *you*," I said.

"After I saved your *life*?"

Damn, it's tough to be a leader these days.

Lessons from Business, and from the Lives of Successful People

In October of 1962, President John Kennedy quoted this poem in a speech he gave in Chicago:

> Bullfight critics row on row
> Crowd the enormous plaza full,
> But only one is there who knows,
> And he is the one who fights the bull.

Kennedy was preoccupied with the loneliness of leadership on that day because the Chicago trip was just a ruse, a red herring of "business as usual" designed to keep America from knowing that a terrible crisis had begun. The Soviets were putting missiles in Cuba.

In the Chicago speech, Kennedy noted that, "Our major problem is the survival of our country, and the protection of its vital interests—*without* the beginning of the third, and perhaps last, war." The day before the speech, Kennedy's advisors had told him that in a nuclear exchange with the Soviets, approximately sixty million Americans, about one-third of the country, would die immediately.

Thus, the stage was set for some of the most wrenching decisions ever made by an American leader.

Kennedy believed that he had only about ten days to resolve the crisis. Once the missiles were *installed*, the global balance of power would shift radically, undercutting America's authority in this issue, and all others.

Kennedy's military advisors, led by General Curtis LeMay, were pushing hard for a surprise, preemptive bombing of Cuba.

But Kennedy refused, primarily because a Pearl Harbor–type bombing raid would violate his vision of America's moral responsibility. As Robert Kennedy put it, "We're not going to make my brother the Tojo of the 1960s."

It was during this week in 1962 that the expression "hawks and doves" was coined, and the "doves," including Robert Kennedy, advocated a naval blockade instead of an attack. They believed that a blockade would prevent nuclear-armed missiles from arriving at the sites.

There was fiery, almost hysterical, debate about the two primary options among Kennedy's closest advisors.

Aide Kenneth O'Donnell asked the president what he would do if the group couldn't reach consensus.

"I'll make my own decision, anyway," Kennedy said. "I'm the one who has the responsibility, so we'll do what I want to do." Then he told O'Donnell that once, at a cabinet meeting, Abraham Lincoln had said, "All in favor, vote aye." The whole cabinet voted "aye." Lincoln voted no, and then announced that the no's had it.

Kennedy "voted" for a blockade.

Kennedy called in a small delegation from Congress and told them about the blockade. One of the congressional leaders told Kennedy that he wanted the record of the meeting to show that JFK had *informed* them about the decision, but had not *consulted* them about it. However, he told the president that he supported him.

After they left, Kennedy remarked angrily, "Oh, sure, we support you, Mr. President, but it's your decision, not ours, and if it goes wrong, we'll knock your block off."

A Soviet freighter carrying the missiles entered Cuban waters. It was turned back by the blockade. But, one way or another, more missiles could be brought in.

With only about forty-eight hours remaining before the missile sites would be ready for the installation of missiles, Kennedy received a letter from the Soviet premier, Nikita Khrushchev. It was conciliatory. Khrushchev offered Kennedy a reasonable compromise. Kennedy went to bed happy.

The next day, another letter from Khrushchev arrived. This one was far more belligerent and proposed unacceptable terms. JFK believed the Soviet Central Committee had drafted the second letter. The letter smacked of the irresponsibility that often comes from committees.

Time was running out. Kennedy had to make the most momentous decision of his life. Arguably, it was the single most important decision in American history.

In a move that was bold, creative, and incisive, Kennedy decided to agree to the conditions of the first, more reasonable letter, and to totally ignore the second letter.

The president and his closest advisor, Robert Kennedy, wrote a note accepting the terms of the first letter. Then Bobby Kennedy, acting as a back-channel negotiator, left the White House to meet with a high-level Soviet representative. He carried the president's note.

While waiting for the response, Kennedy and his friend Dave Powers had a dinner of cold chicken and wine.

Bobby Kennedy returned and said that the Soviets had agreed to their terms. The missile sites would be dismantled.

The president, tremendously relieved, watched Dave Powers nervously gobbling chicken and said, "God, Dave, the way you're eating up all that chicken and drinking up all my wine, anybody would think it's your last meal."

"The way Bobby's been talking," Powers said, "I thought it *was* my last meal."

Everyone laughed. At that point, they could afford to. The decisions were done.

At ease!

Let's relax for a second and take reconnaissance of the ground we've covered so far—because we're at the end of another section.

As we've worked through the various stages of a project, we've found that there are traps and tribulations at every juncture. The planning, training, operations, and maintenance stages of a successful project all require your heart and soul. But now we're moving into the most difficult stage of all: the long-term evolution of an already successful project.

No man knows the future. But you damn well better *try* to know it—as well as you possibly can—or you'll get left behind.

If you can't take your project into the future, it will soon be a thing of the past.

Ready?

Let's hit it!

Shape your own future.

ASK YOURSELF

- Who is the real leader of your company? Is it the highest-ranking person or one of his subordinates? What makes this man the leader?
- When your subordinates have to make sacrifices, do you join them?
- If your boss gave you credit you didn't deserve, would you tell him who really did deserve it?

PART 5

BUILDING ON SUCCESS—
THE ROGUE WARRIOR
WAY

CHAPTER NINE

KILLING COMPLACENCY

"Sweet are the uses of adversity."
—William Shakespeare

"He who stops being better stops being good."
—Oliver Cromwell

"Any coach who doesn't kick the complacent ass on his team will end up kicking his own."

—Pat Riley

Long ago, the great Chinese warrior Sun Tzu conquered a picturesque valley that was rich in food, pure water, and fat livestock, and full of beautiful young peasant girls. He declared that he would use this bountiful territory to conquer his enemy.

Soon, the opposing army, much larger than Sun Tzu's, reached the valley and attacked. Sun Tzu did not commit his army to a full defense. He retreated quickly, in receding waves of troops, and suffered few casualties.

The enemy took over the valley and became entrenched there. They built an encampment, and some of them began to have families with the young women of the area.

Gradually, the enemy of Sun Tzu grew lazy, satisfied, and undisciplined and began to bicker among themselves over the spoils of the valley. Then, after two winters, Sun Tzu's army returned.

Sun Tzu's men were ragged, hungry, and fierce. Sun Tzu surveyed his men and said, "Since a distressed animal will still fight, how much more so will men!"

With great ferocity, Sun Tzu's army attacked. The enemy army, still larger than Sun Tzu's, began to retreat. But Sun Tzu held his men back from pursuit.

Sun Tzu waited until half the enemy army had crossed a river. Then he ordered his army to sweep down upon those who had not yet crossed.

The half of the enemy army that was already across the river did not come to the defense of their comrades. They believed they had escaped, and—because they'd grown soft in this fertile valley—they no longer had the discipline to return to battle. Their generals tried to rally them, to no avail. For two years, the generals had allowed the soldiers to become complacent, and it was too late to undo the damage.

The half of the enemy army that Sun Tzu was attacking fought listlessly. They still thought they might escape—along with their comrades—and they longed to do so.

Sun Tzu's men decimated the first half of the enemy army.

And then they forded the river and destroyed the other half.

When the battle was over, Sun Tzu demanded that his men march away from the valley—quickly and forever.

Even better than he knew the logistics of battle, Sun Tzu knew the minds of men. He knew that all men can be made *complacent* by victory—and that, once they become complacent, they will take the path of least resistance. When this happens, men become lambs ready for slaughter.

This phenomenon has occurred throughout history. Complacency caused the fall of the Roman Empire, and it later contributed to the defeat of the British Empire in colonial America.

In fact, when the newly designed American flag was first raised—on January 1, 1776, in Boston—many of the overconfident and overfed British troops who saw it assumed it was a flag of surrender. They simply could not imagine that the scruffy colonial army led by George Washington would have the *balls* to attack the strongest military force on earth. The British leaders were so overconfident that they did not even plan on committing British troops to the American rebellion. Instead, they planned to use mercenary soldiers from Russia and Germany. This plan remained in effect until March 4, 1776, when the British generals awoke from a long night of drinking and debauchery to find that three thousand American patriots, led by General Washington, had kicked the collective ass of the mercenaries massed in Boston.

More recently, complacency created problems for Israel that *still* undermine the stability of the Middle East. In 1973, the Israeli Defense Forces were still reveling in the cocky afterglow of their victory in the Six Day War of 1967. Since 1967, though, Egypt and Syria had been mercilessly pushing their troops to avenge the humiliation of the Six Day War.

Striking during the Jewish High Holy Days of 1973, Egypt caught Israel napping. Egyptian water cannons blasted sandy fortifications along the Suez Canal until the berms were leveled into landing sites for Egyptian assault boats. Simultaneously, Syrian armored divisions captured portions of the Golan Heights that Israel had arrogantly assumed were safe.

Israel had smugly presumed that its enemies were incapable of these bold and innovative maneuvers. And Israel paid the price, losing land it has never fully regained.

American business, and the American public in general, has been particularly prone to complacency ever since the postwar boom that began in the 1950s. There was great abundance in America after World War II ended, and it had some diabolical side effects. One effect was a tremendous increase in the demand for durable goods, such as cars and appliances, which soon resulted in the manufacturing strategy of "planned obsolescence." Carmakers found that when consumers bought a new car every four or five years, they could get away with building cars that only *lasted* four or five years. Our auto industry became lax, lazy, and greedy and produced shitty cars. Meanwhile, in Japan and Germany—the "defeated" nations—carmakers were learning to build durable cars. And you *know* what happened next.

With the recent globalization of the world's economy, America lost its global dominance. In spite of this, though, many Americans are more complacent than ever. Recent surveys show that items families once considered luxuries, such as second cars and big color TV's, are now widely considered to be necessities. Therefore, American consumers just blithely go out and *buy* all this stuff, and don't worry about *paying* for it. They figure that that's what credit cards are for. Then, when the American consumer gets up to his ass in debt, he just declares bankruptcy or gets on a government program for the "disenfranchised."

It's a shame that we Americans became so complacent from our postwar success because in doing so, we squandered a tremendous amount of momentum. We came out of the Big War with our industrial capacity running at full tilt. If we'd been able to maintain our *motivation*, we'd have kept our momentum, and we would have blown the other industrial nations out of the water. But we got smug, got satisfied, and got our butts kicked.

Instead, we should have tried to constantly *improve*. Evolution comes only through *effort*.

Basketball coach Pat Riley often sees this same squandering of momentum occur in basketball. A team will win a couple of championships, Riley says, and then suddenly all the other teams will roll over and play *dead* whenever the champs come to town. The other teams get fucking *scared* of the champions. So what do the champs do? Often as not, they take their greatness for granted, they screw around, they get fat, and then—*BOOM!*—the real world comes crashing down on them like a million-pound shithammer.

You've got to wage war on complacency every single day. Each new day, you should reinvent your life, striving constantly to make it better than ever. And you've got to remind yourself that you're only as successful as your last success.

One night in a club at Eglin Air Force Base, I met an old top sergeant from World War II who was there for a reunion. I was bitching about the U.S. military getting complacent, and he said, "Hell, over in It-lee, when *my* sons-a-bitches started to feel like they had it made, I'd say, 'Go out and dig a goddamn ditch, and when you're done, fill it up!' Did the same thing with my three boys, when they were growin' up."

"What'd they *get* out of it, your kids?"

"Two of 'em learned the lesson. The other one, he got *strong*. And all three of 'em ended up goin' to college," he said proudly.

"Whatta they doin' now?"

"They ain't diggin' *ditches*," he said.

ROGUETOID: **Do not let success go to your head, or it will soon come out the other end of your anatomy.**

Lessons from War

You may still remember the terrorist hijacking of the *Achille Lauro* cruise ship, but you may not recall a somewhat similar incident that occurred shortly afterward in the Banda Sea of Indonesia, because the government there hushed it up. The Indonesian government, at that time, leaned a little to the right of Hitler concerning freedom of the press. They released about two paragraphs on the incident a month after it happened, so it didn't get much media play. But I remember it. I was there.

The day it happened, my men and I were on a commercial cruise ship in the Bay of Bengal, which is near Indonesia, learning how to deal with future Love Boat hijackings. We didn't want any replays of the *Achille Lauro* goatfuck.

I got word of the hijacking when a three-star admiral choppered in and landed on the deck of our cruise ship. He told me there were two American nationals on the hijacked ship, the *Kyoto Maru*, which was operated by the Indonesians but was owned by a company in Japan. The presence of Americans on the ship didn't exactly give us jurisdiction, but the Indonesians didn't know *what* the hell to do about it, so they'd invited us in. One ranking Indonesian official, the admiral told me, had proposed that they "bomb the ship, and teach the scoundrels a lesson." As I say, the Indonesian government back then was kind of anal retentive about law 'n order.

"We'll handle it," I told the admiral. "One condition. No interference."

"You don't *set* conditions, Captain!" he sputtered.

"Then I guess we're not adequately prepared to volunteer," I said.

The admiral and I went back and forth, but it was just a dance, a dance we'd danced before, and we both knew how it would end.

After the requisite squawking, he gave in and hustled back to his copter. I guess he wanted to get back to the officers' club in Bangkok before his dinner got cold or his daiquiri got warm.

I called the men on deck. But I didn't like what I saw.

The good life on the Love Boat had agreed with these bastards. They'd been eating four-star food and drinking expensive booze. They were relaxed, hung over, and puffy in their guts.

"Coffee break's over, assholes!" I barked. "Time for the real deal."

Before we left the ship, I radioed the Pentagon and got

permission to have an MK-V Special Operations Craft—a real mean-looking gunboat—intercept the *Kyoto Maru* and keep it from leaving its current position. At the moment, it was lodged in a large bay near the Indonesian city of Fakfak, and that's where I wanted it to stay. I wanted the rebels to be as close to land as possible, so that they'd be tempted to escape and abandon the hostages. If they made it out to sea, they'd have no possibility of escape, and they'd fight like trapped animals.

By the time we arrived on the scene, just after nightfall, the gunboat had already prevented the *Kyoto Maru* from leaving Fakfak's harbor. I got on a radio with the rebel honcho, a dickhead named Diwi who called himself a colonel. We immediately nicknamed him Colonel Peewee. He was a Sumatran Communist who was hoping to ignite a nationwide rebellion.

I flattered the pompous Colonel Peewee and did everything I could to make him think he had the upper hand. I wanted him to let down his guard.

First off, I reminded him that *every single hostage* was vitally important to us. I wanted him thinking that he didn't need all 290 of them, which is how many the ship's roster said were on board. Then I kind of hinted that 290 people were going to be a *bitch* to control, and that maybe he'd be in a stronger position if he kept just 30 or 40 of them.

"This is sensible, what you say," he allowed.

I told him his own guys could bring the hostages off. I

said we'd give him a fleet of small speedboats, rafts, whatever he wanted. He seemed to like the idea of having a bunch of boats. Good! I wanted him to feel like he had a practical means of escape. Indonesia consists of hundreds of islands, large and small, and Colonel Peewee probably thought that if he had a fast-enough boat, he could vanish in them like Houdini. I wanted that thought to prey on his mind and weaken his resolve.

Within twenty-four hours, 250 of the passengers were off. Then I started killing Colonel Peewee with kindness. Every time he made a demand, I acquiesced. He wanted to broadcast his "call to arms" to Indonesia, so I gave him broadcast capability on a local radio station. But I cut the station's power down to 250 watts. He was only reaching about a square mile, but we put loudspeakers all around the bay, and it gave the impression that his endless harangues were inundating the countryside.

I kept supplying the ship with the finest food, wine, and liquor that Indonesia had to offer, and I told the ship's captain, who'd stayed aboard, to treat the terrorists like first-class passengers.

When Colonel Peewee demanded money, I sent him some. Of course, I knew he'd have a hard time spending it in hell.

I even sent Peewee some X-rated videotapes and told him I was trying to round up the Real Thing for him, but was having a hard time finding volunteers. He said he understood.

Meanwhile, I was giving my men the exact opposite

treatment. I lodged them in a tenement, cut off their booze, and trained them like dogs. When we hit the ship—and we *would* hit the ship—I wanted them to be mean enough to bite the ass off a bear.

Within a week, Colonel Peewee and his boys were spending most of their time lying in the sun on deck chairs while they listened to a loud, atonal cacophony of Far Eastern music.

On D-day, I staged a fake "rebel attack" on Fakfak. I called down a couple of mortar shots from the hills above the city and staged a miniriot of peasants on the bay front. I "broadcast" a frantic report of the "peasant revolt" on Peewee's radio station. On the ship, Peewee's men were shooting their guns in the air and singing.

That day, they broke out the booze early.

In the middle of the night, after the onboard party ended, we slipped into the water.

We swam silently, our faces painted black, for almost an hour. We towed some of our gear behind us and carried the rest on our backs.

My strongest climber got halfway up the ship by scaling its anchor chain. Then he tossed up a titanium grappling hook to get on deck. He lowered a caving ladder to us, and in less than a minute we were all up. There was no sentry. I guess Colonel Peewee figured we had our hands full fighting the "revolution."

We swept room to room in a carefully choreographed ballet of destruction, using silenced weapons and daggers for the dirty work. The terrorists had each commandeered their own private suites—a stupid move, because it had put them out of communication with one another.

But Peewee himself wasn't quite so stupid. He'd taken a suite with an "escape" door and had barricaded his front door. Before we could throttle him, he took off in the fastest boat he had, a 450-horsepower inboard-outboard with a Volvo outdrive. It was speedier than anything else in the bay.

Except for my helicopter.

Less than a minute after Peewee's untimely departure, Raider was hovering over the Love Boat's deck in the chopper, and I jumped in.

Raider and I were both wearing night-vision goggles, which enabled us to locate Peewee so fast he didn't even have time to shit his pants.

We hit him with a spotlight, and over my loudspeaker, I shouted down, "Trick or treat!" But that didn't seem to ring a bell with him, so I yelled *Stop!* He seemed to know what that meant because he slowed down, aimed an M-60 machine gun at us, and cut loose.

We veered away, picked up some altitude, and then got over him again. I started dropping grenades. The water around him lurched with eruptions. He killed his motor and clasped his hands together, over his head.

"Out of the boat!" I yelled.

When he was in the water, we lowered him a caving ladder.

As he climbed aboard the chopper, he fixed me with a look of superiority.

"We were *so* close," he muttered.

Raider started to laugh.

He laughed so hard I had to take over the controls and fly us back.

Lessons from Business

The Coca-Cola Company *hates* complacency. In Coke's corporate headquarters, it's said that the worst insult that can be leveled at an executive is that "he's *complacent.*"

This contempt for complacency is rooted in the fact that the Coca-Cola Company is in a brutally competitive industry. The international soft drink industry includes not only another giant company, Pepsico, but also dozens of smaller competitors.

However, there are only two significant avenues for marketing Coca-Cola: (1) reaching each new generation, and (2) reaching new markets.

In both of these areas, Coke never rests.

For example, in marketing to a new generation of Japanese Coke drinkers, Coke recently tried the risky strategy of urging kids to drink straight from their Coke bottles—a style of drinking that had always been considered gauche in Japan. The risk paid off. Coke started a national craze called "drinking bugle-style."

In China, Coke decided to reach the younger generation by translating "Coca-Cola" phonetically into Chinese language characters, in order to "speak to the kids in their own language." But the Chinese characters spelled out "Bites the Wax Cowboy." Didn't work. So Coke retooled and renamed their drink "Makes the Mouth Rejoice." Bingo! The kids loved it.

Most of the energy at Coke HQ, though, is dedicated to opening new territories. To achieve this, the chief operating officer at Coke travels about 60 percent of the time, navigating the globe to meet with national directors in intense three-day sessions. At these meetings, says COO John Hunter, "We aren't just batting around ideas. We're talking about action. Fast action! Focused, flexible, and fast!"

A few months after Hunter visits a country, the country's directors come to Coke's Atlanta headquarters to present their one-year and three-year plans and budgets. These Atlanta meetings have been described as "terrifying" and "brutal."

Thus, the attitude at Coke is anything but complacent.

The gung ho attitude at Coke was highlighted when the Berlin Wall came down in 1989. Just hours after the first hammers hit the Wall, a cadre of top Coke executives had left their "war room" in Atlanta and were on their way to Germany. They believed that the first Western soft drink company to establish itself in East Germany would gain a huge advantage over its competitors.

As they flew to Germany, they debated the advisability of even entering the East German market. They estimated that it would require an investment of half a billion dollars. "A lot of people," recalls John Hunter, "were saying, 'East Germany is in a *terrible* economic situation. People who go rushing in with large amounts of money could get *burned.*'"

On the trip over, the executives also brainstormed possible solutions to the most pressing strategic issues— such as whether to let the West German distributor take over East Germany, or to give the territory to someone new.

Shortly after they'd hit the ground, the Coke execs had made their major decisions. In a matter of weeks, Coke was in East Germany. It's now the top-selling soft drink there and generates millions of dollars of profits each month.

Coke knows how to move *fast,* and in business as well as in war, speed is always of the essence.

As much as the Coca-Cola Company hates complacency, though, no one in the world hates it more than Microsoft's Bill Gates. Again, if *anyone* could *afford* to be complacent, it's Gates. He's the richest man in the country, with a fortune of $20 billion. But Gates's hatred for complacency is a major reason *why* he's so rich.

Gates never lets up. "You *always* have to be thinking about who's coming to get you," he says.

Gates urges his top executives to become obsessed with their counterparts at competing companies. He once told them to learn the names of their competitors' kids, and to learn the kids' birthdays.

Jeff Raikes, manager of word processing at Microsoft,

179

took Gates's admonition very seriously and put a picture of his primary competitor's children on his desk. He began sending the kids birthday cards.

"It's a competitive edge we try to hone," Raikes explains. "Bill expected me to always be thinking of my competitor. If you just say, 'We're number one,' that's not good enough."

Gates himself personally visits the offices of his chief competitors' best customers twice each year, demanding to know why they haven't switched their business to *him* yet.

"Success is a lousy teacher," says Gates. "It seduces people into thinking they can't lose. I'm not good at self-congratulation. It has no value. The more successful I am, the more vulnerable I feel. I can't tell you the number of business plans that have been formulated on, 'Hey, we're gonna beat Microsoft.' When you do something well, people expect something *better* the next time."

Gates refuses to indulge in many of the perquisites of success. He doesn't commonly use limousines, chauffeurs, or private jets.

He doesn't even fly first class. Why not? "I'm afraid," he says, "that I'd get used to it."

ASK YOURSELF

- When was the last time you were so committed to a goal that you knew nothing could stop you?

If it was more than five years ago, what's happened to your drive?
- When in your life did you work hardest? Did you
feel more alive then, or now?
- If you achieved your ultimate goal, what would
you do next?

CHAPTER TEN

CHANGE OR DIE

"We have to be able to change, or we will get the hell shot out of us. Nothing ever stays the same in war."
—General George Patton

"Change is happening ten times faster in the 1990s than it did in the 1980s."
—John Neill, CEO of Unipart

"For an enduring organization, there is no finite end state, only a journey—always becoming, never being."
—Gordon R. Sullivan, Former Army chief of staff

I've trained you to fight your business wars with *maximum intensity*—as if there's *no tomorrow*. Well, guess what? There *is* a tomorrow. And it's less than twenty-four hours away.

Are you ready for it? If you're *not*, your business will soon die.

But don't panic. If you've *really learned* how to fight Rogue Warrior style, you already *are* ready for tomorrow. I'll tell you why.

THE ROGUE WARRIOR'S STRATEGY FOR SUCCESS

In learning to fight and succeed Rogue Warrior style, you learned how to be *fast* and *flexible*. And these are the exact qualities that will enable you to build on your success—tomorrow and forever.

As you've read this book, you may have gotten sick of my constant harangue about the importance of certain rules and guidelines. Maybe you wanted more specific advice about *particular aspects* of business strategy. But it's not skill with the *particulars* of business that will ensure your long-term success. The *only* thing that can perpetuate your success into the distant future is strict adherence to a set of tried and true rules.

These rules, which I've referred to as my own "Rogue Warrior rules of engagement," are simple and straightforward.

My personal rules of engagement, as you now know, include the following:

- Aim *before* you shoot.
- Break the rules before they break you.
- *Have* character, but don't *be* a character.
- Lead from the front, where your troops can always see you.
- Don't confuse planning with training, or talking with kicking ass.
- Honor your boundary breakers as much as your boundary makers, because they're your point men.

- Don't be afraid to make mistakes, because the path to glory is littered with fuck-ups.
- Serve a greater cause than your own ego, or you'll be a one-man army.
- Take risks—and then *more* risks.
- Never be satisfied.

These rules of engagement *demand adaptability*, and they *build adaptability*. And adaptability, in the final analysis, is your best protection against the uncertainty of the future.

You cannot control the future. You cannot even *know* the future. All you can do is *anticipate* and *respond* to it. And you will *not* be able to respond successfully unless you are *adaptable*.

If you try to build on your success by creating a company that's too *big* and too *rich* to die, it eventually *will* die. Enormity will no more protect your company than it protected the dinosaurs. It will just invite bureaucracy and rigidity. Richness, alone, will only create passivity and complacency and will soon attract raiders who'll drain your cash and scatter your assets.

If you try to build on your success by designing a company that can *withstand* change—without changing *itself*—it, too, will eventually die. Change is inexorable, and it is irresistible. If you do not *evolve*, you will perish.

Adapting to change is more important now than it's ever been before, because change has recently begun to accelerate. The decentralization of the world's economy, coupled with the advances in information technology, have hastened the pace of change in the marketplace. For example, it's said that in the world of high technology, the "future" now arrives every six months.

Andrew Grove, CEO of Intel, says, "In a world shaped by globalization and the information revolution, there are two options: Adapt or die. The new environment dictates two rules: first, everything happens faster; second, anything that can be done will be done—if not by you, then by someone else. These changes lead to a less kind, less gentle, and less predictable workplace. As managers in such a workplace, you need to develop a higher tolerance for disorder."

As a warrior, I learned to *embrace* disorder and uncertainty. I knew that all uncertainty carried hidden opportunity, and that all disorder held hidden patterns. The trick was to *find* the hidden opportunity and hidden patterns—*before* my enemy did. Often, that wasn't very hard, because—true to human nature—my enemy frequently got all fucked up by disorder and uncertainty.

I might have gotten fucked up myself, if it hadn't been for my strict adherence to the rules I've been telling you about. When I stayed true to my own rules of engagement, I had maximum flexibility, and I could react to change faster and more effectively than my enemy could. Therefore, I could *use* change to defeat him.

As you take your project into the future, you'll find that the future quickly becomes the past. The future is not something that is preordained and is out there waiting for you. The future is whatever you are *making* it, right now. As you shape your present life, you're also shaping your future.

So focus your courage, your heart and soul, and your knowledge on the kind of future you want. Acknowledge your fear, then leave it behind. Forge ahead, embrace change, and *control* change.

Ulysses S. Grant harnessed change to win the Civil War. That war is now seen as the first modern war because it was the first major war fought after the Industrial Revolution. But at the time, nobody knew *what* the hell kind of war it was; they just knew it was different from any other war that had ever been fought.

Before the Civil War, a war could be won by defeating a country's army in a pivotal battle, or series of battles. For example, when Wellington beat Napoleon's army at Waterloo, he beat *France*. But after the Industrial Revolution, a country could not be defeated until its industrial and economic ability to *support* a war was destroyed.

Grant was the first general to fully recognize and respond to this change in warfare. He began attacking not just the South's army but also its industrial capacity. In so doing, he rewrote the rules of warfare, took a calculated risk, and revised his strategy as the war progressed. Thus, Grant prevailed, in part because he was the most *adaptable* general in the war.

In World War II, George Patton also exhibited a hearty appreciation for the importance of not only adaptability but also flexibility. At *any given moment*, Patton was flexible enough to have several contingency plans in place.

Flexibility came naturally to Patton because he was a true Rogue Warrior, who never let bureaucracy and institutional rigidity stop him. He was a man of great character, who made his own rules, took risks, led from the front, learned from his mistakes, and never allowed himself to become complacent.

Patton's greatest contribution to the war came at the Battle of the Bulge. He was pivotally important in turning back the German counteroffensive that almost destroyed the Allied armies.

At the darkest moment of the Battle of the Bulge, a large American force was surrounded by Hitler's fiercest troops, who were demanding surrender. If the Americans surrendered, Germany would be inside the Allied lines, and the invasion of Europe would be stopped.

Eisenhower, Patton, and a few other generals met for an agonizing appraisal of the situation. The surrounded Americans were desperate for reinforcements, supplies, and ammunition. However, a blizzard had begun, paralyzing all units in the area.

But Patton told Eisenhower that he could rescue the trapped army *immediately*. He said, "My Third Army can start moving the minute I call my chief of staff."

The other generals literally laughed. They thought Patton was just grandstanding, because their own units were completely immobilized by the weather and were unprepared for this unforeseen disaster.

But back at Patton's camp, his men were ready to execute several different contingency plans Patton had already devised. All their vehicles were packed, and every few minutes, they started them, to keep the icy weather from freezing their engines. The men were massed together, dressed for battle, and all set to go.

Patton had a number of optional plans, some of which were wholly different from the others. "If we cannot change battle plans," Patton had told his men, "it's the same thing as digging a foxhole where the enemy will find us and put us in our graves. When we're not moving, we're losing."

When the field telephone rang at Patton's camp, his chief of staff picked up the phone, listened to a short order from Patton, and then held up one finger, indicating which battle plan to execute.

On the other end of the phone, at Eisenhower's headquarters, the generals heard the engines at Patton's camp begin to roar. They were dumbfounded.

Eisenhower radioed the commander of the surrounded troops and told him George Patton was on the way.

The commander then sent his reply to the German demand for surrender.

It said, "Nuts."

ROGUETOID: Life is a terminal disease that may overcome you at any moment. What will you do with the next moment of your life?

Lessons from War

There is usually a time in a war when both sides are *certain* they know what the other side will do. Usually, this comes early in the war, before the surprises have begun—and before thousands of brave men have died in missions that were "sure" to succeed.

I remember a time like this in the first conflict I fought in.

After that time, I never indulged in certainty again. There's no point in it. It gets people killed.

These days, I believe in Murphy's Law: Whatever can turn to shit, will turn to shit. In this world, that's as certain as you can get. And the only way to keep from getting fucked up by Murphy's Law is to stay on your toes and be ready for anything.

That was my attitude the day they dropped off my platoon on our last mission of the conflict. This particular conflict was still new to America, but it was old to us. Most of us had been there for months, and it felt like we'd been born there. We were set to be cycled back to the States, but I wanted to get in one last pop before we left. That wasn't the usual attitude, but nothing about me is usual. That's part of the reason I'm still alive.

Our mission was to scout around a small island and look for a weapons cache. The enemy's weapons seemed to be getting better, and Navy intelligence thought this island might be their storage site.

189

A patrol boat dropped us off just before dawn and arranged to pick us up at 2100 on the following day.

The second we got out of the boat, the surprises began. As I hopped into the chest-deep water, my feet were sucked eighteen inches into the mud. By the time we struggled to shore, our weapons and supplies were clogged with gluey brown silt. We scrambled into the underbrush to disassemble our equipment and clean it. As I took my rifle apart, I whispered, "I hope to Christ they don't attack now."

But they did. Murphy's fucking Law.

We shot back with the few functional weapons we had, then ran like sons of bitches through the muck and undergrowth. We managed to carry off some of our stuff but lost most of it.

We ran until we lost the enemy, then collapsed, gasping for air. The jungle had sliced us open, and flies were going after our steamy blood.

Shit! In thirty minutes, we'd gone from being hunters to being the hunted.

Our radio was broken. We were on our own.

I thought that maybe one of our men could swim to shore, which was two miles away, so I sent out my strongest swimmer. But as soon as he was 250 meters offshore, we heard the scream of a jet engine. A jet fighter swooped down on my man with its guns blasting. My guy dove and eluded the plane, which wasn't at its best strafing lone swimmers. When my guy crawled back onto our beach, he was white and shaky.

"Looks like Plan B," I said.

"What's Plan B?" asked Mickey Kalosh.

"Survival," I said. "We gotta stay alive 'til our boat gets back."

I surveyed the men. Nobody looked scared. Just focused. These guys were tough and smart, and now their character was the primary element that stood between them and death.

"We better *try* some shit," said Mickey Kalosh, "or these people will get us *runnin'*, and leavin' tracks, and then they'll kill us for sure."

"You read my mind," I said. "Never defend; always attack."

"Attack with *what*, Lieutenant?" asked Raider. "We don't have *dick* for weapons."

"With whatever we can scrounge."

We found a main trail and left our broken radio on it. But not before we'd booby-trapped it with our last fragmentation grenade.

We disappeared back into the bush. Then we heard the grenade go off, accompanied by a yelp. "Let's stay *after* 'em," I said. "I wanna find their camp."

We walked toward the highest point on the island, but the mud sucked down our legs until they burned with exhaustion. "Who's got an idea about this mud?" I asked.

"I do," said a kid we called Doc. "Skis. We lash palm fronds to our boots and ski right over the top of this shit."

"Try it," I said.

It didn't work.

But Mickey modified it and came up with contraptions that looked like snowshoes. Damned if they didn't work.

As night fell, we dined on rainwater, snake, and raw bird's eggs. From the top of a tree, I spotted a needle of light that was probably a campfire. I got a fix on the location. In the morning, we'd visit it.

By 0600, we were on a bluff overlooking their camp. Raider, who had our only binoculars, spotted their weapons cache. It was a long slit-trench covered with tree limbs. The weapons sat in it on a makeshift scaffolding, just out of the water that collected in the bottom of the trench.

"Holy shit!" Raider whispered when they pulled off some of the tree limbs. "They got *everything!*"

It was an impressive storehouse of ordnance. They had Chinese rifles, Soviet AK-47s, mortar shells, boxes of grenades, C-4 plastic explosives, inflatable boats, M-60 machine guns, Soviet rocket-propelled grenades—you name it. Made my mouth water. Only problem was, they were doubtless going to use some of it to try to kill us.

"Let's break into pairs and play sniper," I said. "Give 'em a taste of their own medicine. On this island, on this day, *we're* the guerrillas, and *they're* the superior, better-equipped force, so we've gotta adjust. Don't engage in firefights. Just hit and run. Keep 'em off balance and confused, and meet at the boat just before twenty-one hundred." Everybody was clear eyed and calm. Another day at the office.

All day long, I heard isolated cracks of gunfire. I got off

192

a few shots myself. When I got down to my last six bullets, I stopped sniping.

After dark, the men began to collect near the pickup site. We had one last job to do.

I knew that when the boat came, it would probably draw the enemy to the area. So, using our rifles and knives, we dug a two-foot-deep pit in the trail that led to the pickup site. We sharpened stakes and pushed them into the pit, pointed end up. We stuck our knife handles into the floor of the pit and covered the top of it with palm leaves and grass.

Then we waded into the water, crouched nose deep, and waited.

The boat was on time. But as the low groan of its motor approached from the distance, we heard a commotion from the bush. *Everybody* had heard the boat.

The enemy was getting closer by the second. I could hear individual voices.

But then I heard a high-pitched "Eehh!" and a moan. It was followed by another wail of pain.

The boat rushed up to us and got between us and the shore. From the shore, there was a halfhearted volley of fire—just enough to go *ping* on the side of the boat.

After all of my men were on, I swung myself over the stern. The boat surged off, and I lay on my back, panting hard, gazing at the stars overhead, reveling in the feeling of safety.

The boat's chief looked down at me. "Home, James," I said.

As we headed back, I radioed the base and called down an air strike on the weapons cache. I wanted to take it out before the enemy got a chance to move it.

I saw one of our planes soar overhead, and then I heard a loud *BOOM!* and saw light rise over the island.

The men and I watched the light rise together. It was a moment of great camaraderie—but not our first, and sure as hell not our last. Years later, I would recruit many of these same men for my famed SEAL Team Six.

I wanted these guys to stay with me because they were extraordinary men. They hadn't been trained specifically for counterterrorism, but in this conflict, they'd learned to roll with the punches, improvise, and adapt—and with these qualities, they could adjust to *any* job.

When we got back to camp, it seemed as if everybody there was waiting for us. They knew where we'd been, they'd heard what had happened, and they wanted to see which of us was still alive.

Sometimes, back then, after a particularly hairy mission, when a patrol would return to base, they would come back in single file, with the leader going first, and everybody else arranged in order of rank and seniority.

Not this time. Not for our last mission. As we came through the gate, into the middle of the crowd of men who were waiting for us, I slowed down until everyone had caught up.

Then we all walked through together, shoulder to shoulder, eight men abreast—leaders all—headed back home, and headed into the future.

194

When I was debriefed, I told an intelligence officer about the weaponry I'd seen, including the jet.

Long story short, he thought I was crazy—or "functionally traumatized," as he put it. He said the enemy just didn't *have* the resources I claimed to have seen.

Later on, he—and the entire U.S. government—found out otherwise. The enemy had all the resources it needed.

Still, even after it had *seen* the new reality, the U.S. command kept fighting the enemy the same way as before.

They weren't flexible. They didn't change.

And they didn't win.

Lessons from Business

You'd think that if your company ever hit the fabled Fortune 500 list, it would finally be *safe*. You could kick back, put the company on autopilot, and just keep *doing what you do*. After all, if your company is one of the five hundred biggest corporations in America, you've got it made, right?

Wrong.

Companies *drop off* the *Fortune* 500 list with *alarming* regularity. Every decade, one-third of the companies on the list fall off. And the turnover rate has been accelerating every year.

Current success is absolutely no guarantee of *future*

success. If you don't believe me, take a look at the recent histories of the companies that were featured in the 1982 business classic *In Search of Excellence.* That book described forty-three companies with excellent track records.

However, just five years after that book was published, only fourteen of those forty-three companies still retained their previous level of success, and eight were in serious financial trouble.

Any company that has fallen from grace has its own particular tales of bad luck and bad decisions. Most of them, though, have one thing in common: They didn't *respond effectively to change.*

Often as not, the *world changed,* but *they didn't.*

They weren't flexible. Instead of bending, they broke.

A good example of a company that was badly damaged by inflexibility is the communications conglomerate ITT. ITT was once one of the elite high-tech companies in the world. In 1980, ITT owned 250 subsidiary companies, with sales of $22 billion. It employed 400,000 people.

ITT was run by Harold Geneen, who was considered one of the shrewdest managers in the world. Geneen had created a vastly diversified company out of what had once been just a collection of telecommunications firms.

Geneen's basic strategy was to buy a wide *variety* of companies—which sold everything from Twinkies to fire hydrants—in order to spread his risks. His companies had varying earnings cycles and were in widely diverging industries, so ITT's combined cash flow was steady and dependable.

Because ITT's many acquisitions had generated tremendous debts, Geneen pushed each of his individual company managers hard, insisting that they make enough profit to help pay down the debt. For the most part, they met his demands.

But the whole strategy turned to absolute shit. As Geneen focused on squeezing as much as possible from each of his companies, his overall empire floundered.

Geneen left ITT with a $5 billion debt, and annual interest payments of $600 million.

What had gone wrong? Only one thing. Times had changed. ITT hadn't.

In the 1970s, Geneen's strategy had worked well because the economy was growing quickly. Because of this rapid expansion of business, ITT could effectively pay down its debt with profits. Also, the high inflation of the 1970s diminished ITT's debt.

However, in the 1980s, the economy contracted and inflation leveled off. When this happened, ITT's debt became a crushing burden.

However, ITT did not expeditiously respond to the changing business environment. The company was complacent, stuck with the "old rules," and refused to adapt.

ITT wasn't flexible, fast, or focused.

And it lost its position as one of America's great companies.

A company that *did* change, before it was too late, was General Electric. At the beginning of the 1980s, GE had become a slow, rigid bureaucracy. Like ITT, it was run under an old-fashioned system of highly centralized power. The corporate staff was immense and unwieldy; in many divisions, it reached a depth of nine management layers.

Instead of being driven by the desires of its *customers*—as are most great retail companies these days—GE was driven by a system of *financial* management.

The finance division had twelve thousand employees, representing 8 percent of GE's workforce. The financiers were not risk takers, innovators, or men of vision. Their primary goal was to track profits efficiently and keep from making mistakes.

Because of its cumbersome and unresponsive structure, GE quickly fell behind in the most exciting new areas of electronics, such as mobile communications, robotics, and computers. For a while, it looked as if GE might be sold off piecemeal and would soon cease to exist.

But GE turned itself around. How? They didn't do it with a great technological breakthrough or a dramatic merger. They did it the simple way: A new leader came in and kicked ass. The new leader, Jack Welch, grabbed the power from the bean counters in finance and started taking risks, rewriting GE's corporate rules of engagement, and leading from the front.

Welch decimated GE's bureaucracy. This enhanced the company's speed and allowed it to quickly recover from any mistakes that might have resulted from taking risks.

Almost immediately, GE became more responsive to its customers' needs and more innovative in consumer electronics.

GE became a flexible, adaptable company that evolved gracefully as the years passed. Now GE is stronger than ever and has become the kind of company that can increase its success forever.

One of the most flexible companies in America, though, is Wal-Mart, which was the vision of the great Sam Walton. Walton started with just one store in rural Arkansas in the early 1960s and eventually became the most successful retailer in the world, with over 330,000 employees. When he died in 1992, he was the richest man in the United States, worth over $30 billion.

Wal-Mart's incredible success was partly the result of its ability to adapt to change. Sam Walton ran his company Rogue Warrior style, and this endowed the company with great adaptability and flexibility.

How was Sam Walton a Rogue Warrior?

He was a Rogue Warrior because he was a man of enormous *character,* who created not just a company, but a *cause.* His cause was the "retail meritocracy," in which all employees were treated with equal respect and given the opportunity to become leaders themselves. Walton *dictated the rules of engagement* not just to his own employees but also to his major competitors—chiefly Sears and Kmart—and when his rules were no longer serving him, he *rewrote them.* He *led from the front, planned carefully,* and was zealous about properly *train-*

ing his employees. He *took risks* and quickly *learned from his mistakes.* And Sam Walton never became *complacent,* even after he was richer than God and Donald Trump put together.

The unpretentious Walton always led from the front, and he joined his men in the trenches. Once, he was feeling restless in the middle of the night, so he got out of bed and bought fifty doughnuts from an all-night bakery. He took them down to the loading dock of one of his stores and spent the night talking to the crews. Walton, whose own executive suite was as Spartan as a warehouse, felt totally at home with his "shooters." While he was on the loading dock, he found out his men needed two more shower stalls. So he took care of it himself the next morning. This was when his sales were approaching $25 billion annually.

Walton hated bureaucracy and did everything possible to empower his people at the grassroots level. His motto was, "Think small." He broke each of his enterprises into small teams of self-managed people. For example, in every store, he established proprietorships in each department; he called them "stores within a store." He believed in, as he put it, "pushing responsibility down, and pushing ideas up."

Above all, Walton was responsive to his *customer.* He said, "There is only one boss: the customer. And he can fire everybody in the company, from the chairman on down, simply by spending his money somewhere else."

Because of these values, which kept Walton in close contact with every corporate undercurrent and every consumer trend, Walton was better able than his competitors to *know* when *change* was occurring. He was also better able to *adapt* to change. And he was better able to *inaugurate* change.

He initiated a major change in American retailing when he gave birth to the concept of "everyday discount pricing." This revolutionary concept rewrote the rules of retailing and gave rise to what is now a huge segment of the retail marketplace.

In the 1970s and 1980s, however, the proliferation of indoor shopping malls threatened the success of one-stop shopping stores, like Wal-Mart and Sears. These malls provided the same variety and convenience as the large one-stop stores, by linking together a number of smaller stores and boutiques. Sears suffered terribly from this phenomenon and lost its position as America's leading store. But Wal-Mart responded to this change in American shopping habits by aligning itself in formal economic partnerships with its major suppliers, such as Proctor & Gamble—a strategy no other megastore chain had ever tried. With these partnerships, Wal-Mart was able to beat every other one-stop chain, and all boutiques, on price and selection. During this time, Wal-Mart vaulted past not only Sears but also Kmart.

Mostly though, Wal-Mart used its speed and flexibility in thousands of *little* ways, day in and day out, in accordance with Walton's dictum of "Think small." For example, if Walton learned that Kmart was planning to build a store in a new area, Walton would immediately build *two* Wal-Marts in the area before Kmart could mobilize its bureaucracy. Almost always, this stopped Kmart's incursion.

In the final analysis, though, it was what was *inside Walton himself* that made his company great. For the last story in this book, let's return to one of the subjects that *started* the book: character.

Character has to be at the absolute *core* of all your enterprises. To begin any project, you have to have a *leader* with character who builds a *team* with character. If you don't have that, the project will be stillborn.

But to carry your project to a successful conclusion, you need to *retain* character—right to the end. Sam Walton did.

In 1991, Sam Walton was dying of bone cancer. He was weak and in pain, and was seventy-three years old. Nonetheless, he still flew his own twin-prop Cessna to store after store.

As he slowly climbed into the plane one day, on his way to visit a new Wal-Mart in Ohio, he told an old friend, "There are still about thirty Wal-Marts I've never been to. I've got to get to 'em *soon*."

His friend began to protest.

Walton cut him off.

"I don't want Wal-Mart going *soft*," Walton said. "Do *you*?"

Although Sam Walton is dead now, Wal-Mart— created in Sam Walton's image—is still the world's leading retailer.

Under a bold new leader, Wal-Mart still operates Rogue Warrior style.

THE ROGUE WARRIOR'S STRATEGY FOR SUCCESS

Wal-Mart has learned how to *perpetuate* its success.
For Wal-Mart, *the future is now.*

You and I are now at the end of our tour of duty. I hope you got something out of it.

If you've been paying attention, you should now be able to successfully ramrod a project through its various stages.

You should know by now that in the *planning* stage of the project, you've got to set tough but realistic goals, devise smart strategies, and dictate the rules of engagement.

In the *training* stage, you've got to build a team with character and train them so relentlessly that the real thing will feel like a *vacation.*

In the *operational* phase, you've got to be willing to make mistakes, learn from them quickly, and then rewrite the rules of engagement in accordance with what you've learned.

Then, to *maintain* your success, you've got to continue to take risks, including the biggest risk of all—leading your people from the front, where your *own* ass is on the line.

And, finally, you should know that to *perpetuate* your success into the future, you've got to keep from being complacent, you've got to keep evolving, and you've got to maintain maximum flexibility and adaptability.

If you know all this, there's nothing more I can do to prepare you.

You're ready.

I wish you good luck and Godspeed. Your battles will be painful. The enemies you engage will be fierce.

But if you bring a warrior's heart into battle, you will not only survive, *you will prevail*.

Ready to engage?

ENGAGE!

References

The following sources were consulted in the research of this book.

Warren Bennis, *On Becoming a Leader*, Addison-Wesley Publishing Co., New York, 1989.

Warren Bennis and Burt Nanus, *Leaders*, Harper & Row, New York, 1985.

Jim Bishop, *F.D.R.'s Last Year*, Pocket Books, New York, 1975.

Robert Caro, *The Years of Lyndon Johnson—Path to Power*, Alfred A. Knopf, New York, 1982.

Roger Cohen and Claudio Gatti, *In the Eye of the Storm*, Farrar, Straus and Giroux, New York, 1991.

Peter Collier and David Horowitz, *The Fords*, Summit Books, New York, 1987.

Col. Larry R. Donnithorne, *The West Point Way of Leadership*, Doubleday, New York, 1993.

Charles Farkas and Phillipe DeBacker, *Maximum Leadership*, Henry Holt and Co., New York, 1996.

REFERENCES

James J. Flexner, *Washington*, Little, Brown and Co., New York, 1969.

Martin Gilbert, *Churchill*, Henry Holt and Co., New York, 1991.

David Halberstam, *The Reckoning*, William Morrow & Co., New York, 1986.

Gary Heil, Tom Parker, and Rick Tate, *Leadership and the Customer Revolution*, Van Nostrand Reinhold, New York, 1995.

Thomas R. Horton, *The CEO Paradox*, American Management Association, New York, 1992.

Harvey Mackay, *Swim with the Sharks*, William Morrow & Co., New York, 1988.

William Manchester, *American Caesar*, Little, Brown and Co., New York, 1982.

Robert Merriam, *Battle of the Bulge*, Ballantine Books, New York, 1957.

Earl S. Miers, *Robert E. Lee*, Alfred A. Knopf, New York, 1956.

Emmett C. Murphy, *The Genius of Sitting Bull*, Prentice Hall, New Jersey, 1993.

Frank Pacetta with Roger Gittines, *Don't Fire Them, Fire Them Up*, Simon & Schuster, New York, 1994.

Tom Peters, *Liberation Management*, Ballantine Books, New York, 1992.

Tom Peters and Robert Waterman, *In Search of Excellence*, Warner Books, New York, 1982.

REFERENCES

Tom Peters, *Thriving on Chaos*, Random House, New York, 1987.

Tom Peters, *A Passion for Excellence*, Random House, New York, 1985.

Donald T. Phillips, *Lincoln on Leadership*, Warner Books, New York, 1992.

Lou Pritchett, *Stop Paddling and Start Rocking the Boat*, HarperCollins Publishers, New York, 1995.

Colin Powell with Joseph E. Persico, *My American Journey*, Random House, New York, 1995.

William Richards, *The Last Billionaire: Henry Ford*, Charles Scribner's Sons, New York, 1948.

Pat Riley, *The Winner Within*, G.P. Putnam's Sons, New York, 1993.

Robert Michel, *Strategy Pure & Simple*, McGraw Hill, New York, 1993.

Gordon R. Sullivan and Michael V. Harris, *Hope Is Not a Method*, Random House, New York, 1996.

J. B. Strasser and Laurie Becklund, *Swoosh*, Harcourt Brace Jovanovich, New York, 1991.

Sun Tzu, *The Art of War*, Westview Press, Boulder, Colorado, 1994.

Dave Thomas with Ron Beyma, *Well Done!* HarperCollins Publishers, New York, 1994.

James Wallace and Jim Erickson, *Hard Drive*, John Wiley & Sons, New York, 1992.

REFERENCES

Sam Walton with John Huey, *Made In America*, Doubleday, New York, 1992.

Thomas J. Watson Jr., and Peter Petre, *Father Son & Co.*, Bantam, New York, 1990.

Randall P. White, Philip Hodgson, and Stuart Crainer, *The Future of Leadership*, Pitman Publishers, Lanham, Maryland, 1996.

Porter B. Williamson, *Patton's Principles*, Simon & Schuster, New York, 1982.

Bob Woodward, *The Commanders*, Pocket Books, New York, 1991.